Gaslighting Manipulation

Identifying, Understanding and Escaping Psychological Manipulation

Dr. Evelyn Harper

© 2022 by Dr. Evelyn Harper - All rights reserved.

Table of contents

Introduction: 4

Chapter 1: What Is Gaslighting? The Subtle Art of Control 7

Chapter 2: The Anatomy of a Gaslighter 27

Chapter 3: How to Recognize Gaslighting in Real-Time 53

Chapter 4: The Impact of Gaslighting on Your Mental Health 79

Chapter 5: Breaking the Cycle: Setting Boundaries and Saying No 106

Chapter 6: Escaping Gaslighting Relationships 132

Chapter 7: Rebuilding Your Identity and Confidence 159

Chapter 8: Living Gaslight-Free: Maintaining Healthy Relationships 188

Chapter 9: The Role of Society: Gaslighting in Media and Culture 216

Chapter 10: Gaslighting Recovery Toolkit 244

Conclusion: 271

References 275

Author Name: Dr. Evelyn Harper 279

Disclaimer: 281

Copyright 282

Legal Notice 283

Introduction:

Breaking Free from the Shadows of Gaslighting

Imagine living in a world where your thoughts, feelings, and memories are constantly called into question. You feel like you're walking through a fog, second-guessing your every decision, and wondering if you're the one losing touch with reality. This is the insidious reality of gaslighting—a form of psychological manipulation that creeps into your life and erodes your sense of self.

Gaslighting isn't just a word; it's a silent epidemic. It can occur in romantic relationships, families, workplaces, friendships, and even in the media and politics. Its effects are far-reaching, leaving victims feeling confused, powerless, and trapped in a web of doubt. Yet, despite its prevalence, many people struggle to recognize gaslighting when it happens and often blame themselves for the turmoil they experience.

This book is your beacon of light in the darkness—a guide to uncovering, understanding, and escaping the shadow of gaslighting. Whether you're just beginning to suspect that you've been a victim of manipulation or you're ready to take the final steps toward breaking free, this book is here to empower you with the knowledge and tools you need to reclaim your life.

Why This Book?

The subject of gaslighting has been widely discussed, but many resources only scratch the surface. This book dives deeper, offering not only theoretical insights but also practical strategies that you can apply immediately to regain your sense of self and build a gaslight-free future. While other books may leave you with a better understanding of the problem, this one provides a clear roadmap to recovery and resilience.

What You'll Discover

In these pages, you'll find:

- **Clarity:** A clear explanation of what gaslighting is, how it works, and why it's so effective at controlling others.
- **Recognition:** Tools to identify gaslighting in all its forms—whether it's happening in your personal relationships, at work, or even on a societal level.
- **Empowerment:** Strategies to confront gaslighters, set boundaries, and break free from toxic relationships.
- **Healing:** Practical steps to rebuild your confidence, rediscover your identity, and cultivate healthy relationships moving forward.

This isn't just a book about recognizing manipulation; it's a manual for transformation. You'll emerge from this journey stronger, wiser, and equipped to protect yourself from manipulation in the future.

Who This Book Is For

This book is for anyone who has ever felt trapped in a cycle of manipulation and self-doubt. It's for those who have questioned their reality, blamed themselves for conflicts they didn't create, or stayed in relationships that felt toxic but inexplicably hard to leave. It's also for the friends, family members, and allies who want to understand gaslighting and support their loved ones in overcoming it.

Whether you're seeking to escape an abusive relationship, recover from emotional wounds, or simply educate yourself about psychological manipulation, this book will meet you where you are and guide you toward the life you deserve.

A Journey of Self-Discovery

Escaping gaslighting isn't just about identifying and confronting manipulators. It's also about rediscovering who you are without the fog of manipulation clouding your mind. Throughout this book, you'll embark on a journey of self-discovery, learning to trust your intuition, honor your feelings, and reclaim your power.

The road ahead won't always be easy, but every step will bring you closer to freedom. By the end of this book, you'll not only understand gaslighting but also feel equipped to break free from its grip and thrive in a world where your truth is your greatest strength.

Chapter 1: What Is Gaslighting? The Subtle Art of Control

Imagine this scenario: You tell a friend about an event that deeply hurt you, only for them to dismiss it, saying, "That never happened. You're imagining things." Or perhaps you confront a partner about a behavior that upset you, and they respond, "You're too sensitive; it's not a big deal." Over time, these seemingly minor interactions pile up, leaving you doubting your perception, your emotions, and even your sanity.

This is gaslighting—a psychological tactic used to manipulate someone into questioning their own reality. The term originated from the 1938 play *Gas Light* (and its subsequent film adaptations), where a husband manipulates his wife into believing she's losing her mind. The title comes from his act of dimming the gas lights in their home while insisting to his wife that the lights remain unchanged. The term has since become synonymous with a pattern of control and manipulation designed to destabilize and disempower.

Defining Gaslighting in Clear Terms

At its core, **gaslighting is a form of psychological abuse** that aims to make someone question their perception of reality. It's a subtle and insidious tactic that often goes unnoticed until significant damage has been done. Unlike overt forms of abuse, gaslighting operates covertly, making the victim feel as though they're the problem rather than the perpetrator.

Key elements of gaslighting include:

1. **Distortion of Reality:** The manipulator denies, distorts, or reframes events to suit their narrative.
2. **Erosion of Confidence:** The victim begins to doubt their memory, judgment, and sanity.
3. **Control:** The ultimate goal of gaslighting is to gain power over the victim by destabilizing their sense of self.

How Gaslighting Works

Gaslighting is not a single act but a series of calculated behaviors designed to confuse and control. These tactics often occur gradually, making it harder for victims to recognize them. Here are common methods gaslighters use:

1. Denial

The gaslighter outright denies events or conversations ever took place. For example:

- "I never said that. You're imagining things."
- "That's not how it happened. You're making it up."

2. Minimization

The gaslighter downplays the victim's feelings or experiences, making them seem insignificant:

- "You're overreacting."
- "It wasn't that bad. Stop being so dramatic."

3. Diversion

The gaslighter shifts the focus to avoid accountability:

- "You're always so sensitive. Why can't you take a joke?"
- "Are you sure this isn't about your insecurities?"

4. Projection

The gaslighter accuses the victim of the very behavior they're exhibiting:

- "You're the one manipulating me."
- "Stop trying to control everything."

5. Creating Doubt

The gaslighter plants seeds of doubt in the victim's mind:

- "Are you sure that's what happened? You've been so forgetful lately."
- "Maybe you're just tired and misremembering."

The Psychological Impact of Gaslighting

The effects of gaslighting are far-reaching and deeply damaging. Over time, victims may experience:

1. **Confusion and Self-Doubt:** Victims begin to distrust their own perceptions, leading to chronic uncertainty.
2. **Erosion of Self-Esteem:** Constant invalidation can make victims feel incompetent and unworthy.

3. **Anxiety and Depression:** The emotional toll of gaslighting often manifests as mental health struggles.
4. **Isolation:** Gaslighters often alienate their victims from support systems, making them feel alone and dependent.
5. **Learned Helplessness:** Victims may feel powerless to change their situation, believing they're at fault for the abuse.

Why Gaslighting Is So Insidious

Gaslighting is uniquely harmful because it operates in the gray areas of communication and relationships. Unlike physical abuse, which leaves visible scars, gaslighting attacks the mind, making it harder to detect and confront. Some of the reasons it's so effective include:

1. **Incremental Nature:** Gaslighting often begins subtly, with small denials or dismissals that escalate over time.
2. **Emotional Manipulation:** Gaslighters exploit the victim's vulnerabilities and emotions, making them feel complicit in their abuse.
3. **Social Perception:** Gaslighters often appear charming or reasonable to outsiders, making it difficult for victims to seek validation or support.
4. **Undermining Reality:** By targeting the victim's perception of reality, gaslighters strip away their ability to trust themselves or others.

Real-Life Examples of Gaslighting

1. **In Romantic Relationships:** A partner consistently denies flirting with others, despite clear evidence, and accuses their significant other of being jealous and paranoid.
2. **In the Workplace:** A manager takes credit for an employee's work, then insists the employee is imagining things when confronted.
3. **In Families:** A parent dismisses a child's feelings by saying, "You're making a big deal out of nothing," even when the child is expressing genuine hurt.
4. **In Society:** Media outlets or political figures deny facts or historical events, creating confusion and division among the public.

Recognizing the Red Flags

Gaslighting can be difficult to identify, especially when it's happening in a close relationship. However, some warning signs include:

- Feeling like you're always apologizing, even when you haven't done anything wrong.
- Frequently questioning your memory or judgment.
- Feeling isolated from friends or family due to the manipulator's influence.
- Experiencing a sense of unease or confusion in the presence of the gaslighter.

A Historical Overview of Gaslighting

Gaslighting, a term now widely used in psychology and popular discourse, has its roots in a fictional narrative that starkly illustrates the power of manipulation. Over the years, its meaning has evolved to describe a pervasive form of psychological abuse that affects individuals, relationships, and even societies. To fully grasp the concept and its relevance today, we must trace its origins and explore its historical development.

The Origin of the Term

The term "gaslighting" originates from the 1938 British play *Gas Light*, written by Patrick Hamilton, which was later adapted into two films, most notably the 1944 American version starring Ingrid Bergman and Charles Boyer. The story revolves around a husband who manipulates his wife into believing she is losing her sanity. He achieves this by subtly altering their environment—most famously, dimming the gaslights in their home—and denying the changes when she notices them. This calculated denial of reality, combined with other psychological manipulations, gradually makes the wife doubt her perceptions, memory, and mental stability.

The narrative struck a chord with audiences, as it showcased a chillingly effective form of abuse that relies on deception and control rather than overt violence. The play and films popularized the term "gaslighting," which soon entered psychological and cultural lexicons to describe similar behaviors in real life.

Early Use in Psychology

The term began to gain traction in psychological circles in the mid-20th century as a way to describe a specific form of emotional abuse. Early research into gaslighting focused on its effects within intimate relationships, particularly in cases of domestic abuse. Psychologists observed that perpetrators often used tactics similar to those depicted in *Gas Light*—denying facts, rewriting history, and undermining the victim's sense of reality—to maintain control.

During the 1960s and 1970s, as awareness of domestic violence grew, gaslighting was increasingly recognized as a tool abusers used to isolate and dominate their victims. However, it wasn't until the late 20th century that the term began to be applied more broadly to other types of relationships, including workplace dynamics, friendships, and societal manipulation.

Gaslighting and Feminist Movements

The feminist movements of the 1960s and 1970s played a pivotal role in bringing attention to gaslighting as a form of emotional abuse. Activists highlighted how gaslighting was often used to silence and discredit women, particularly in patriarchal systems that dismissed women's experiences and emotions as "irrational" or "hysterical."

In this context, gaslighting was identified not just as an interpersonal dynamic but also as a systemic issue. For example:

- Women who reported domestic abuse were often met with disbelief and told they were exaggerating or imagining things.
- Workplace discrimination and harassment were frequently downplayed or denied, leaving women questioning their own experiences.

This period marked a significant shift in how gaslighting was understood, linking it to broader social and cultural patterns of power and control.

Gaslighting in Sociopolitical Contexts

Gaslighting is not limited to personal relationships; it has also been employed on a societal level. Governments, organizations, and media have used gaslighting tactics to manipulate public perception and maintain power. Historical examples include:

- **Propaganda Campaigns:** Authoritarian regimes have often relied on gaslighting techniques, such as denying atrocities, rewriting history, and spreading disinformation to confuse and control the populace. For example, during Stalin's rule in the Soviet Union, purges and show trials were accompanied by denials and distortions that left citizens doubting their own observations.
- **Civil Rights and Activism:** Movements for equality have frequently been met with gaslighting. Activists are often dismissed as "troublemakers" or accused of exaggerating injustices, a tactic designed to undermine their credibility and suppress dissent.

- **Modern Politics:** The term has seen a resurgence in recent years, with commentators using it to describe political strategies that involve blatant denial of facts, reframing of events, and manipulation of public discourse.

The Digital Age and the Evolution of Gaslighting

In the 21st century, the digital age has given gaslighting new dimensions. Social media, fake news, and disinformation campaigns have created fertile ground for mass gaslighting. Key developments include:

- **Online Manipulation:** Troll farms and bot accounts spread false narratives, creating confusion about what is real and what is fabricated.
- **Gaslighting in Relationships:** Digital communication has made it easier for gaslighters to control their victims, using tactics such as denying messages or manipulating shared information.
- **Media and Cultural Gaslighting:** News outlets and influencers may perpetuate gaslighting by denying truths or selectively framing stories to fit specific agendas.

Gaslighting in Popular Culture and Awareness

As awareness of gaslighting has grown, it has become a topic of interest in popular culture, psychology, and self-help literature. Books, movies, and television shows increasingly depict gaslighting scenarios, helping audiences recognize and understand its dynamics. Examples include:

- Psychological thrillers like *Gone Girl* and *Big Little Lies*, which explore manipulative relationships.
- Discussions in self-help and mental health communities that provide tools for identifying and countering gaslighting.

This growing awareness has also led to the inclusion of gaslighting in mental health diagnostics and therapy. Today, therapists and counselors are trained to recognize the signs of gaslighting and help clients rebuild their confidence and trust in their perceptions.

Real-Life Anecdotes: How Gaslighting Unfolds in Different Scenarios

Gaslighting manifests in various areas of life, from personal relationships to professional settings, and even within families. Below are fictionalized anecdotes, crafted to protect privacy, that vividly illustrate how gaslighting operates in relationships, workplaces, and families. These stories not only highlight the tactics used but also reveal the emotional toll and confusion victims often face.

1. Relationships: Love Turned to Control

The Case of Emma and Liam
Emma and Liam had been together for two years when subtle changes began to creep into their relationship. Initially, Liam was attentive and affectionate, but over time, his behavior shifted.

One evening, Emma confronted Liam about a text message she'd seen on his phone from an unfamiliar number. The message seemed overly friendly, bordering on flirtatious. When Emma asked about it, Liam laughed it off.

"Oh, Emma, are you being paranoid again? You always do this," he said, his tone dismissive.

Emma, feeling guilty for snooping, apologized. Yet, the texts continued, and Liam's explanations grew more elaborate. When Emma mentioned her concerns a second time, Liam raised the stakes:

"You've always been insecure, haven't you? Maybe you should talk to someone about that."

Emma began to doubt her instincts. Was she really insecure? Was she imagining the tone of the messages? Over the months, Liam's tactics escalated. He dismissed her concerns, rewrote past conversations, and accused her of trying to control him. Emma, once confident, now felt like a shadow of herself—unsure of her perceptions, her feelings, and even her worth.

Impact: Liam's gaslighting eroded Emma's self-confidence and ability to trust her own instincts. She felt trapped in a cycle of doubt, questioning whether she was the problem in the relationship.

2. Workplace: Undermining and Isolation

The Case of David and His Manager, Claire
David, a marketing associate, had always been diligent and

innovative in his work. His new manager, Claire, seemed supportive at first, often praising his ideas during team meetings. However, things changed after David proposed a bold new campaign.

Claire subtly began to undermine him. She'd assign tasks to him without clear instructions and then criticize him for not meeting her expectations. When David asked for clarification, she would respond, "I told you exactly what to do—are you not paying attention?"

During one project meeting, Claire interrupted David mid-sentence, stating, "That's not what we agreed on." Confused, David checked his notes and emails but found nothing to suggest he'd misunderstood. He approached Claire privately, but she dismissed his concerns:

"David, you've been so forgetful lately. Are you sure everything's okay with you?"

Over time, Claire escalated her tactics. She'd attribute David's successful ideas to other team members and accuse him of being defensive when he spoke up. By the end of the quarter, David was doubting his competence and wondering if he was truly as inattentive as Claire suggested.

Impact: Claire's gaslighting left David questioning his professional abilities. The constant invalidation and blame created a hostile work environment, eroding his confidence and morale.

3. Families: A Parent's Subtle Manipulation

The Case of Sarah and Her Mother, Evelyn
Growing up, Sarah always felt that her mother, Evelyn, had a way of twisting things. When Sarah expressed hurt or disappointment, Evelyn would respond with phrases like, "You're too sensitive," or, "I never said that—you're making it up."

As Sarah got older, she began noticing patterns. One Thanksgiving, Sarah brought up a childhood memory of being scolded unfairly in front of relatives. Evelyn immediately denied it:

"That never happened, Sarah. You've always been dramatic."

The rest of the family laughed it off, but Sarah felt humiliated. Later, when she tried to talk to her mother about it, Evelyn turned the tables:

"Why do you always bring up the past? I've done so much for you, and this is how you repay me?"

The guilt worked. Sarah found herself apologizing, even though she still felt hurt. These incidents continued into adulthood, with Evelyn often dismissing Sarah's feelings and rewriting family events to suit her narrative. Sarah began to doubt her recollections and avoided conflict, even when her mother's actions caused pain.

Impact: Evelyn's gaslighting created a dynamic where Sarah felt silenced and invalidated. This eroded Sarah's confidence in her own memories and made it difficult for her to set boundaries.

Common Themes Across These Scenarios

These anecdotes reveal several common elements of gaslighting:

- **Denying Reality:** In each case, the gaslighter denies events or feelings, leaving the victim questioning their memory and perception.
- **Rewriting History:** Gaslighters often revise past events to fit their narrative, further confusing the victim.
- **Blaming the Victim:** The gaslighter shifts responsibility, making the victim feel at fault for the conflict or manipulation.
- **Isolating the Victim:** Gaslighting creates doubt and insecurity, which can isolate victims from seeking support.

Gaslight Glossary: Understanding the Language of Manipulation

Gaslighting operates in the shadows of communication, using subtle tactics to distort reality and erode confidence. To effectively identify and counteract gaslighting, it's essential to understand the terminology and psychological concepts that underpin this form of manipulation. Below is a unique **"Gaslight Glossary"**, a curated list of terms that explain the tactics and dynamics often employed by gaslighters.

1. Projection

- **Definition:** The act of attributing one's own thoughts, feelings, or behaviors to another person, often to deflect blame or guilt.
- **Example in Gaslighting:** A gaslighter may accuse you of being dishonest when they are the ones lying. By projecting their actions onto you, they shift attention away from their own behavior.
- **Impact:** Victims often feel defensive and confused, questioning whether they are truly at fault.

2. Emotional Invalidation

- **Definition:** Dismissing or undermining someone's feelings, making them feel as though their emotions are unimportant or irrational.
- **Example in Gaslighting:** When you express sadness or frustration, the gaslighter responds with, "You're overreacting," or, "Stop being so sensitive."
- **Impact:** Over time, victims may suppress their emotions, doubting whether their feelings are valid or acceptable.

3. Cognitive Dissonance

- **Definition:** The mental discomfort experienced when holding two conflicting beliefs, values, or perceptions.
- **Example in Gaslighting:** A gaslighter may treat you with affection one moment and criticize you harshly the next. This inconsistency creates confusion and makes it difficult to reconcile their behavior with your perception of the relationship.

- **Impact:** Victims often feel trapped, oscillating between self-doubt and the hope that the manipulator's kind behavior reflects their "true self."

4. Reality Twisting

- **Definition:** The deliberate distortion of facts or events to fit the gaslighter's narrative.
- **Example in Gaslighting:** When you confront a gaslighter about a specific incident, they insist, "That's not what happened," or, "You're remembering it wrong."
- **Impact:** Victims begin to question their memory and perception, relying increasingly on the gaslighter's version of events.

5. Blame Shifting

- **Definition:** Redirecting responsibility for an issue or conflict onto the victim to avoid accountability.
- **Example in Gaslighting:** After being caught in a lie, the gaslighter says, "You're always trying to find something wrong with me. This is your fault for being so suspicious."
- **Impact:** The victim feels guilty and responsible, even when they've done nothing wrong.

6. Gaslighting by Proxy

- **Definition:** Involving a third party to reinforce the gaslighter's narrative or invalidate the victim's perspective.

- **Example in Gaslighting:** A gaslighter might say, "Even [third party] agrees that you're imagining things," or manipulate others into doubting the victim's credibility.
- **Impact:** Victims feel further isolated and powerless, as the manipulator enlists others to validate their distorted reality.

7. Selective Amnesia

- **Definition:** Pretending to forget or denying events that occurred, especially when they reflect poorly on the gaslighter.
- **Example in Gaslighting:** "I don't remember saying that. Are you sure you're not confusing me with someone else?"
- **Impact:** Victims question their memory and may avoid bringing up past issues for fear of being dismissed.

8. Token Gestures

- **Definition:** Small acts of kindness or affection used to manipulate the victim into staying in the relationship or doubting their concerns.
- **Example in Gaslighting:** After a heated argument, the gaslighter surprises you with a thoughtful gift or a romantic gesture, making you second-guess your perception of their toxicity.
- **Impact:** Victims feel conflicted, believing the gaslighter's kind moments may outweigh their harmful behavior.

9. Triangulation

- **Definition:** The use of a third person to create conflict, confusion, or competition in a relationship.
- **Example in Gaslighting:** The gaslighter says, "Even [third party] thinks you're overreacting," or compares you unfavorably to another person to make you feel inadequate.
- **Impact:** Victims feel alienated, insecure, and increasingly dependent on the gaslighter for validation.

10. Manipulative Reframing

- **Definition:** Changing the context or interpretation of an event to make the victim appear unreasonable or at fault.
- **Example in Gaslighting:** If you express hurt over a gaslighter's comment, they might respond, "I was just joking—you can't take anything seriously."
- **Impact:** Victims feel dismissed and may start to doubt their ability to interpret interactions correctly.

11. Splitting

- **Definition:** Viewing people or situations in extremes, such as all good or all bad, often to manipulate perceptions.
- **Example in Gaslighting:** The gaslighter idolizes you one moment and demonizes you the next, saying things like, "You're perfect," followed by, "You're the reason everything goes wrong."

- **Impact:** Victims experience emotional whiplash, struggling to understand their standing in the gaslighter's eyes.

12. Mirroring

- **Definition:** Mimicking the victim's behaviors, values, or interests to build trust and create a false sense of connection.
- **Example in Gaslighting:** A gaslighter pretends to share your goals and dreams but later dismisses or sabotages them, saying, "You're not cut out for this."
- **Impact:** Victims feel betrayed and question the authenticity of their relationship with the gaslighter.

13. The Fog Effect

- **Definition:** Creating confusion and uncertainty by providing mixed messages or inconsistent behavior.
- **Example in Gaslighting:** The gaslighter alternates between affection and criticism, leaving you unsure where you stand or what to expect.
- **Impact:** Victims feel emotionally paralyzed, unable to make decisions or take action.

14. Escalation

- **Definition:** Increasing the intensity of manipulation when the victim begins to resist or question the gaslighter's behavior.

- **Example in Gaslighting:** When you call out their actions, the gaslighter responds with anger or exaggerated accusations to distract and overwhelm you.
- **Impact:** Victims may retreat, feeling too exhausted or intimidated to continue challenging the gaslighter.

Chapter 2: The Anatomy of a Gaslighter

Gaslighting is not just a random act of manipulation—it is a deliberate, calculated strategy employed by individuals who seek control, dominance, or validation at the expense of others. To understand gaslighting fully, it's essential to dissect the anatomy of a gaslighter: their psychology, motivations, tactics, and behavioral patterns.

This chapter explores what drives gaslighters, how they operate, and why their tactics are so effective.

Who Are Gaslighters?

Gaslighters can be anyone—a partner, friend, family member, coworker, or even a public figure. While gaslighters come from all walks of life, certain personality traits and psychological factors are common among them:

1. **Narcissistic Tendencies:** Many gaslighters exhibit narcissistic traits, such as an inflated sense of self-importance and a deep need for admiration. Gaslighting serves as a tool to maintain their superiority and manipulate others into validating their ego.
2. **Insecurity and Fragility:** Beneath their confident facade, gaslighters often harbor deep insecurities. By undermining others, they deflect attention from their vulnerabilities and create a sense of control.
3. **Sociopathic or Machiavellian Traits:** Some gaslighters are more calculating and lack empathy, seeing manipulation as a means to achieve their goals. These

individuals are often skilled at exploiting others without remorse.
4. **Learned Behavior:** Gaslighting can also stem from upbringing or past experiences. Those who grow up in manipulative environments may unconsciously adopt similar behaviors, seeing them as normal or necessary.

What Motivates Gaslighters?

Gaslighting is a means to an end, driven by various motivations:

1. **Control and Power:** Gaslighters often seek to dominate their relationships by controlling the victim's perceptions and actions. By making the victim doubt their reality, the gaslighter becomes the ultimate authority.
2. **Self-Preservation:** Gaslighting can serve as a defense mechanism. For example, a gaslighter may deny wrongdoing or shift blame to protect their image or avoid accountability.
3. **Validation and Ego Boost:** Gaslighters thrive on feeling superior. Undermining others reinforces their belief in their own intellectual, emotional, or moral superiority.
4. **Avoidance of Vulnerability:** Gaslighting allows individuals to avoid confronting their own flaws, fears, or failures by projecting these onto their victims.
5. **Entertainment or Malice:** In extreme cases, gaslighters may manipulate others for amusement or out of a sense of malice, taking pleasure in the confusion and pain they cause.

How Gaslighters Operate: Common Tactics

Gaslighters use a range of tactics to manipulate their victims and maintain control. These behaviors are often subtle, making them difficult to detect. Here are some of the most common methods:

1. Denial of Reality

- Gaslighters refuse to acknowledge events or conversations, even when presented with evidence.
- Example: "I never said that. You must be imagining things."

2. Emotional Invalidations

- They dismiss or belittle the victim's feelings, making them feel irrational or overly sensitive.
- Example: "You're too emotional. Calm down."

3. Rewriting History

- Gaslighters alter past events to fit their narrative, creating confusion and self-doubt.
- Example: "That's not how it happened. You're remembering it wrong."

4. Blame Shifting

- They redirect responsibility for their actions onto the victim, making them feel at fault.

- Example: "You're always making me angry. This is your fault."

5. Isolation

- Gaslighters may isolate their victims from friends and family to increase dependence.
- Example: "Your friends don't really care about you. I'm the only one who understands you."

6. Love-Bombing and Token Gestures

- Periodic affection or compliments are used to keep the victim invested in the relationship.
- Example: "You know I only do this because I love you."

7. Triangulation

- Involving a third party to validate the gaslighter's narrative or undermine the victim.
- Example: "Even [third person] agrees that you're overreacting."

The Psychology Behind Gaslighting

Gaslighting is rooted in psychological manipulation, exploiting vulnerabilities in the victim's cognition and emotions. Key psychological principles at play include:

1. **Cognitive Dissonance:** Victims experience discomfort when their reality conflicts with the gaslighter's narrative. Over time, they may reconcile this dissonance

by accepting the gaslighter's version of events, even when it contradicts their own experiences.
2. **Learned Helplessness:** Repeated invalidation and blame cause victims to feel powerless, believing they cannot change their circumstances.
3. **Intermittent Reinforcement:** Gaslighters alternate between affection and manipulation, creating a cycle of hope and confusion that keeps the victim invested.
4. **Exploitation of Trust:** Gaslighters often target individuals who trust them deeply, making it easier to manipulate their perceptions and emotions.
5. **Mirror Neurons and Empathy:** Victims often empathize with the gaslighter, interpreting their behavior as unintentional or stemming from pain. This empathy makes it harder for the victim to recognize manipulation.

Case Studies: Gaslighters in Action
Romantic Partner:

A manipulative partner accuses their significant other of infidelity while secretly cheating themselves. This deflection shifts focus away from their wrongdoing and keeps the victim on the defensive.

Boss:

A toxic manager regularly dismisses an employee's ideas, only to present them as their own in meetings. When confronted, they claim, "I had this idea before you even mentioned it."

Parent:

A controlling parent denies ever criticizing their child, even when confronted with specific examples. "I would never say something like that. You're twisting my words."

The Long-Term Impact of Gaslighting

Gaslighting leaves deep scars, including:

- **Erosion of Self-Esteem:** Victims often feel inadequate and incapable of making sound judgments.
- **Chronic Anxiety:** Constant doubt and confusion take a toll on mental health.
- **Difficulty Trusting Others:** Victims struggle to trust relationships, fearing further manipulation.
- **Identity Crisis:** Years of gaslighting can cause individuals to lose their sense of self, unsure of their values, preferences, and goals.

Psychological Profiles of Common Gaslighter Archetypes

Gaslighters come in various forms, each employing unique strategies to manipulate and control others. While their tactics may differ, their core motivations—power, control, and validation—are often the same. Understanding the psychological profiles of common gaslighter archetypes can help you recognize and counteract their behaviors. Below are some of the most prevalent archetypes and their defining traits.

1. The Power Seeker

- **Core Motivation:** Domination and control.
- **Personality Traits:**
    - Authoritarian and controlling.
    - Thrives in hierarchical relationships (e.g., workplaces, family dynamics).
    - Dismissive of others' autonomy and boundaries.
- **Tactics:**
    - Uses fear and intimidation to assert dominance.
    - Denies others' achievements while inflating their own authority.
    - Rewrites history to maintain control over narratives.
- **Example:**
    - A controlling boss who consistently undermines employees' confidence, ensuring they feel incompetent and dependent on their leadership.
- **Psychological Insights:**
    - Power Seekers often have deep-seated insecurities and fear losing authority. Their gaslighting serves as a way to mask these vulnerabilities.

2. The Manipulative Narcissist

- **Core Motivation:** Validation and self-enhancement.
- **Personality Traits:**
    - Inflated sense of self-importance.
    - Lack of empathy.
    - Seeks admiration and approval at all costs.
- **Tactics:**

- Dismisses or diminishes others' perspectives to reinforce their own superiority.
- Uses charm and charisma to disarm victims initially, only to manipulate them later.
- Engages in projection, accusing others of the very flaws they exhibit.
- **Example:**
    - A romantic partner who insists their significant other is "too sensitive" when confronted about hurtful comments, all while demanding constant praise for their "honesty."
- **Psychological Insights:**
    - Narcissists often rely on gaslighting to maintain their carefully constructed self-image. By invalidating others, they avoid facing their own flaws.

3. The Perpetual Victim

- **Core Motivation:** Sympathy and avoidance of responsibility.
- **Personality Traits:**
    - Plays the victim to gain attention and support.
    - Avoids accountability for their actions.
    - Skilled at eliciting guilt from others.
- **Tactics:**
    - Reframes conflicts to position themselves as the aggrieved party.
    - Accuses others of mistreatment to deflect from their own manipulative behavior.
    - Uses guilt as a tool to control others' actions.
- **Example:**

- A family member who insists, "After everything I've done for you, this is how you repay me," when asked to respect boundaries.
- **Psychological Insights:**
    - Perpetual Victims use gaslighting as a defense mechanism, shielding themselves from criticism by shifting blame onto others.

4. The Charismatic Sociopath

- **Core Motivation:** Personal gain and control over others.
- **Personality Traits:**
    - Charming and persuasive.
    - Lacks empathy or remorse.
    - Highly strategic and manipulative.
- **Tactics:**
    - Uses charm to gain trust and establish control.
    - Denies or twists facts to serve their agenda.
    - Employs triangulation, involving third parties to validate their perspective and isolate the victim.
- **Example:**
    - A coworker who spreads false rumors about you while acting as your ally, saying, "Everyone thinks you're overreacting, but I'm on your side."
- **Psychological Insights:**
    - Sociopaths view relationships as opportunities for manipulation. Their charm masks their true intent, making them particularly dangerous gaslighters.

5. The Overbearing Parent

- **Core Motivation:** Maintaining control over their child's life and decisions.
- **Personality Traits:**
    - Overprotective and intrusive.
    - Believes they know what's best, often to the detriment of the child's autonomy.
    - Struggles to respect boundaries.
- **Tactics:**
    - Dismisses the child's feelings or achievements with phrases like, "You'll understand when you're older."
    - Rewrites family history to justify their actions.
    - Uses guilt to manipulate the child into compliance.
- **Example:**
    - A parent who denies ever making critical remarks, saying, "I only want what's best for you. If you feel hurt, that's on you."
- **Psychological Insights:**
    - Overbearing parents often gaslight out of fear of losing influence. Their manipulation is rooted in their struggle to let go as their child becomes independent.

6. The Passive-Aggressive Gaslighter

- **Core Motivation:** Indirectly asserting control without confrontation.
- **Personality Traits:**
    - Avoids direct conflict.

- Uses sarcasm and veiled insults.
            - Relies on ambiguity to maintain plausible deniability.
    - **Tactics:**
        - Makes hurtful comments disguised as jokes: "You're so sensitive—can't you take a joke?"
        - Denies responsibility by claiming, "That's not what I meant. You're reading too much into it."
        - Plants seeds of doubt subtly, leaving the victim questioning their interpretation.
    - **Example:**
        - A friend who consistently makes dismissive remarks about your achievements but insists, "I'm just teasing. You know I support you."
    - **Psychological Insights:**
        - Passive-aggressive gaslighters often struggle with expressing emotions directly. Their gaslighting is a way to avoid vulnerability while maintaining control.

7. The Opportunistic Gaslighter

- **Core Motivation:** Achieving short-term goals, often at the victim's expense.
- **Personality Traits:**
    - Pragmatic and self-serving.
    - Flexible in their tactics, adapting to the situation.
    - Often lacks a long-term agenda.
- **Tactics:**
    - Capitalizes on moments of vulnerability to manipulate others.

- Uses selective memory or denial to escape accountability.
- Discards relationships once they are no longer useful.
- **Example:**
  - A colleague who denies agreeing to help with a project, leaving you to shoulder the workload alone, then takes credit for its success.
- **Psychological Insights:**
  - Opportunistic gaslighters prioritize personal gain over relationships, often leaving a trail of confusion and broken trust in their wake.

8. The Jealous Saboteur

- **Core Motivation:** Undermining others to satisfy their envy.
- **Personality Traits:**
  - Deeply insecure and competitive.
  - Resents others' success or happiness.
  - Skilled at masking their envy with concern or criticism.
- **Tactics:**
  - Undermines the victim's confidence with backhanded compliments or subtle critiques.
  - Dismisses or sabotages the victim's goals, often framing it as "realistic advice."
  - Spreads doubt among others to isolate the victim.
- **Example:**
  - A friend who says, "Are you sure you can handle that promotion? It seems really stressful," while secretly hoping you'll decline.

- **Psychological Insights:**
  - Jealous Saboteurs use gaslighting to level the playing field, diminishing others' achievements to mask their own insecurities.

Insights into the Vulnerabilities Gaslighters Exploit

Gaslighting is a calculated and manipulative behavior that preys on specific vulnerabilities within individuals. By identifying and understanding these vulnerabilities, gaslighters gain the upper hand, weaving doubt, confusion, and dependency into the victim's psyche. This chapter explores the types of vulnerabilities gaslighters exploit, how they identify them, and why they are so effective in maintaining control.

1. Emotional Sensitivity and Empathy

Gaslighters often target individuals who are emotionally sensitive and empathetic because these qualities can be weaponized against them.

- **How They Exploit This Vulnerability:**
  - By framing their manipulative actions as unintentional or as a result of their own pain, gaslighters appeal to the victim's empathy.
  - They use the victim's desire to understand and help as a way to deflect attention from their abusive behavior.
  - Statements like, "You're overreacting; I didn't mean to hurt you," or "You know how hard things have been for me," can make empathetic

individuals feel guilty for confronting the gaslighter.
- **Why It's Effective:**
    - Empathetic individuals often prioritize the feelings of others over their own, making it harder for them to hold the gaslighter accountable.
    - They may hesitate to set boundaries, fearing they might seem unkind or uncaring.

2. Low Self-Esteem and Insecurity

Individuals with low self-esteem or self-doubt are particularly vulnerable to gaslighting, as they are already predisposed to questioning their own worth and judgment.

- **How They Exploit This Vulnerability:**
    - Gaslighters amplify existing insecurities by criticizing or dismissing the victim's thoughts, feelings, or abilities.
    - They often position themselves as the "voice of reason," making the victim feel dependent on their guidance and validation.
    - Comments like, "You're lucky to have someone like me to keep you grounded," or, "If you were more confident, you wouldn't make such mistakes," deepen the victim's self-doubt.
- **Why It's Effective:**
    - Victims with low self-esteem are more likely to internalize the gaslighter's negative feedback, reinforcing their belief that they are flawed or inadequate.

- The gaslighter becomes a source of validation, making it harder for the victim to break away.

3. Desire for Approval

The need for approval and validation from others can be a powerful vulnerability that gaslighters exploit to their advantage.

- **How They Exploit This Vulnerability:**
    - Gaslighters use the victim's need for approval as leverage, offering praise and acceptance only when it suits their agenda.
    - They may alternate between approval and criticism to keep the victim striving for their validation.
    - Phrases like, "If you really cared about me, you wouldn't question me," manipulate the victim's need for acceptance into compliance.
- **Why It's Effective:**
    - Victims become trapped in a cycle of seeking the gaslighter's approval, which can feel like an emotional reward.
    - The intermittent reinforcement of praise keeps the victim attached to the relationship, even when it is toxic.

4. Fear of Conflict

Gaslighters often exploit individuals who dislike confrontation or fear conflict, as these individuals are less likely to challenge manipulative behavior.

- **How They Exploit This Vulnerability:**
    - Gaslighters escalate conflicts or employ emotional outbursts to intimidate the victim into silence.
    - They frame disagreements as personal attacks, making the victim feel guilty for bringing up concerns.
    - Statements like, "You're always trying to start a fight," discourage the victim from addressing issues.
- **Why It's Effective:**
    - Victims who fear conflict may avoid standing up for themselves to maintain peace, allowing the gaslighter to continue their behavior unchecked.
    - This avoidance further isolates the victim, as they suppress their concerns and emotions.

5. Trust and Loyalty

Gaslighters thrive in relationships where trust and loyalty are significant because these values can be manipulated to their advantage.

- **How They Exploit This Vulnerability:**
    - Gaslighters position themselves as the victim's confidant, fostering a sense of dependence and loyalty.
    - They twist the victim's trust by denying actions or statements, knowing the victim is less likely to question them.
    - They may say, "If you loved me, you'd trust me," to dissuade the victim from doubting them.

- **Why It's Effective:**
  - Victims are less likely to suspect manipulation from someone they trust, giving the gaslighter greater freedom to distort reality.
  - Loyalty to the gaslighter can make the victim feel conflicted about seeking help or walking away.

6. Past Trauma or Abuse

Individuals with a history of trauma or abuse are more susceptible to gaslighting because their previous experiences may have already eroded their sense of self-worth and reality.

- **How They Exploit This Vulnerability:**
  - Gaslighters use triggers from past trauma to destabilize the victim emotionally, keeping them in a state of fear or confusion.
  - They may mimic patterns of previous abuse, reinforcing the victim's feelings of helplessness or inevitability.
  - Phrases like, "No one else will put up with you," or, "You should be grateful for what you have," prey on the victim's fear of abandonment.
- **Why It's Effective:**
  - Victims with unresolved trauma may already struggle with self-doubt, making them more likely to accept the gaslighter's version of events.
  - Gaslighting compounds the psychological wounds of past trauma, further eroding the victim's sense of reality and agency.

7. Isolation or Lack of Support

Gaslighters often target individuals who are isolated or lack a strong support system, as these individuals are easier to manipulate without external perspectives.

- **How They Exploit This Vulnerability:**
    - Gaslighters intentionally isolate their victims, cutting them off from friends, family, or other sources of support.
    - They may say, "Your friends don't really care about you," or create conflict with the victim's loved ones to deepen the isolation.
    - Without external validation, the victim becomes increasingly reliant on the gaslighter for their sense of reality.
- **Why It's Effective:**
    - Isolation leaves the victim without a sounding board, making it easier for the gaslighter to distort their perceptions and experiences.
    - The lack of support reinforces the victim's dependence on the gaslighter, deepening the cycle of manipulation.

8. Guilt and Responsibility

Gaslighters exploit a victim's sense of responsibility or tendency to feel guilt, using these emotions to shift blame and avoid accountability.

- **How They Exploit This Vulnerability:**

- They frame their actions as the victim's fault, saying things like, "You made me do this," or, "If you hadn't acted that way, I wouldn't have reacted like this."
    - They use the victim's guilt to manipulate them into apologizing or making amends, even when they've done nothing wrong.
- **Why It's Effective:**
    - Victims who take on blame or responsibility are more likely to accept the gaslighter's narrative and less likely to confront them.
    - Guilt keeps the victim in a state of emotional vulnerability, making it easier to control them.

Interactive Exercise: Spot the Tactic

Gaslighting is often subtle and insidious, making it difficult to recognize in real-time. This interactive exercise, **"Spot the Tactic,"** is designed to help you identify manipulative behaviors by presenting realistic scenarios where gaslighting may occur. By analyzing each example, you'll learn to recognize the red flags and understand the specific tactics being used.

How It Works

1. **Read the Scenario:** Each example will describe a situation involving potential gaslighting.
2. **Identify the Tactic:** Think about what manipulative behavior is being demonstrated.
3. **Reflect:** After each scenario, we'll break down the tactic, its psychological purpose, and its potential impact.

Scenario 1: Denial and Rewriting History

Situation:
You remind your partner, Jamie, about a conversation you had last week where you both agreed to attend a family dinner on Friday. Jamie responds with:

"I don't remember that at all. You must be mixing things up. We never talked about that, and besides, I'm pretty sure I told you I had other plans."

Question:
What tactic is Jamie using here?

Analysis:

- **Tactic:** Denial and rewriting history.
- **Purpose:** By denying the conversation and reframing events, Jamie shifts the blame to you for the misunderstanding. This creates doubt in your memory and perception.
- **Impact:** You may begin to question your recollection, feeling confused and hesitant to assert yourself in the future.

Scenario 2: Emotional Invalidation

Situation:
At work, you tell your manager, Claire, that you're feeling overwhelmed by your current workload. Claire responds with:

"Everyone else on the team is handling it just fine. Maybe you're just not cut out for this kind of role."

Question:
What tactic is Claire using?

Analysis:

- **Tactic:** Emotional invalidation.
- **Purpose:** Claire dismisses your feelings and attributes your struggles to a personal shortcoming. This undermines your confidence and discourages you from expressing concerns again.
- **Impact:** You may internalize the criticism, believing you're at fault for not meeting expectations, even if the workload is genuinely unreasonable.

Scenario 3: Projection

Situation:
Your roommate, Alex, accuses you of being messy and not cleaning up after yourself, even though you've consistently done your share of chores. You notice Alex frequently leaves dirty dishes in the sink and forgets to take out the trash.

Question:
What tactic is Alex using?

Analysis:

- **Tactic:** Projection.

- **Purpose:** By accusing you of their behavior, Alex diverts attention away from their actions and puts you on the defensive.
- **Impact:** You may feel obligated to prove your cleanliness or take on more responsibilities to avoid further accusations.

Scenario 4: Blame Shifting

Situation:
You confront your sibling, Taylor, about borrowing your belongings without asking. Taylor responds with:

"Maybe if you weren't so uptight about your stuff, I wouldn't feel like I have to sneak around. You're the one creating this problem."

Question:
What tactic is Taylor using?

Analysis:

- **Tactic:** Blame shifting.
- **Purpose:** Taylor avoids accountability by making you feel responsible for their actions. This shifts the focus away from their behavior and onto your alleged rigidity.
- **Impact:** You may feel guilty and question whether you're being unreasonable, even though your boundary is valid.

Scenario 5: Gaslighting by Proxy

Situation:
After an argument, your friend, Maya, tells you:

"Even Sarah agrees that you overreacted. Maybe you should think about why so many people think you're too emotional."

Question:
What tactic is Maya using?

Analysis:

- **Tactic:** Gaslighting by proxy.
- **Purpose:** Maya uses a third party's supposed opinion to validate their perspective and invalidate your feelings. Whether Sarah actually agrees or not is irrelevant—the mention of her name adds weight to Maya's argument.
- **Impact:** You may feel isolated and question whether others perceive you as Maya claims, further undermining your confidence.

Scenario 6: Token Gestures

Situation:
After weeks of dismissive and critical comments, your partner, Sam, surprises you with a thoughtful gift and says:

"I've been under a lot of stress lately, but I hope you know how much you mean to me."

Question:
What tactic is Sam using?

Analysis:

- **Tactic:** Token gestures.
- **Purpose:** By offering a small act of kindness, Sam distracts from their previous behavior and creates confusion about their intentions. This makes it harder for you to address their consistent mistreatment.
- **Impact:** You may feel conflicted, wondering if you've been misinterpreting their actions or if their behavior is justified because of stress.

Scenario 7: The Fog Effect

Situation:
Your colleague, Chris, frequently gives you unclear instructions for projects. When you ask for clarification, Chris says:

"I've already explained this twice. Maybe you should pay more attention during our meetings."

Question:
What tactic is Chris using?

Analysis:

- **Tactic:** The fog effect.
- **Purpose:** Chris creates confusion by providing vague instructions, then shifts the blame to you for not

understanding. This undermines your confidence and discourages you from seeking clarity in the future.
- **Impact:** You may start to doubt your abilities and feel reluctant to ask questions, leaving you more susceptible to Chris's control.

Scenario 8: Triangulation

Situation:
Your partner, Jordan, compares you unfavorably to a mutual friend, saying:

"Why can't you be more like Sarah? She never complains about small things like this."

Question:
What tactic is Jordan using?

Analysis:

- **Tactic:** Triangulation.
- **Purpose:** Jordan introduces a third party as a comparison to make you feel inadequate and gain the upper hand in the relationship.
- **Impact:** You may feel insecure and strive to meet unrealistic standards to regain Jordan's approval.

Reflect and Apply

By identifying gaslighting tactics in these scenarios, you build the awareness needed to recognize manipulation in your own life. Take a moment to reflect:

- Did any of these scenarios feel familiar?
- How would you respond differently now that you understand the tactic being used?
- What boundaries or strategies could you use to protect yourself in similar situations?

Chapter 3: How to Recognize Gaslighting in Real-Time

Gaslighting often begins subtly, weaving manipulation into daily interactions so seamlessly that victims may not notice its presence until the damage has been done. Recognizing gaslighting in real-time is crucial for regaining control, protecting your sense of reality, and taking steps to address the behavior. This chapter equips you with practical tools and strategies to identify gaslighting behaviors as they occur, enabling you to respond confidently and assertively.

1. Understand the Common Signs of Gaslighting

To recognize gaslighting in real-time, familiarize yourself with the telltale signs. Here are some common behaviors to watch for:

a. Denial of Reality

- **What It Looks Like:** The gaslighter denies events, conversations, or agreements, even when evidence exists.
- **Example:** "That never happened. You're imagining things."

b. Emotional Invalidation

- **What It Looks Like:** They dismiss or minimize your feelings, making you question their validity.
- **Example:** "You're overreacting. Stop being so sensitive."

c. Blame Shifting

- **What It Looks Like:** They deflect responsibility by making you feel at fault for their actions.
- **Example:** "If you hadn't acted that way, I wouldn't have reacted like this."

d. Rewriting History

- **What It Looks Like:** The gaslighter changes past events to suit their narrative, creating confusion.
- **Example:** "I never said that. You're twisting my words."

e. Contradictory Statements

- **What It Looks Like:** They frequently change their story or contradict themselves to sow doubt.
- **Example:** "I never said that" followed later by "You misunderstood what I meant."

2. Pay Attention to Your Emotional Responses

Your emotions can be powerful indicators that gaslighting is happening. Here are some common feelings to watch for and their implications:

- **Confusion:** You feel disoriented or unsure about what's real or true.
- **Self-Doubt:** You begin questioning your memory, perception, or instincts.
- **Guilt:** You feel overly responsible for the other person's emotions or actions.

- **Fear or Anxiety:** You feel hesitant to bring up concerns, fearing you'll be dismissed or invalidated.

Action Step: When these feelings arise during an interaction, pause and ask yourself:

- "What specifically is making me feel this way?"
- "Is this a pattern I've noticed before?"

3. Develop a Gaslighting Checklist

A checklist can help you identify gaslighting behaviors in real-time. Use the following questions to assess whether an interaction may involve gaslighting:

1. **Are they denying something I know to be true?**
2. **Are they dismissing my feelings as irrational or invalid?**
3. **Do I feel confused, guilty, or defensive after talking to them?**
4. **Are they blaming me for something they did?**
5. **Are they twisting past events to suit their narrative?**

If you answer "yes" to multiple questions, there's a strong possibility gaslighting is at play.

4. Recognize Gaslighting Patterns

Gaslighting is rarely a one-time occurrence; it often unfolds as a repeated pattern of behaviors. Recognizing these patterns in real-time involves:

- **Journaling Interactions:** Keep a record of conversations or incidents where you felt confused or invalidated. Look for recurring themes.
- **Identifying Cycles:** Gaslighters often alternate between manipulation and affection to keep you invested. If you notice this cycle, it's a red flag.
- **Tracking Emotional Shifts:** Note if you consistently feel worse about yourself after interacting with a specific person.

Example: If you notice that every time you express an opinion, the person dismisses it and later blames you for the disagreement, this pattern could indicate gaslighting.

5. Strengthen Your Inner Voice

Gaslighting thrives on making you doubt yourself. Strengthening your confidence in your own perceptions is a powerful defense.

Practice Reality Affirmations

- **What It Looks Like:** Silently affirm your experience when the gaslighter tries to distort it.
- **Example:** "I know what I saw. Their denial doesn't change the facts."

Seek External Validation

- If you're unsure whether your perception is accurate, consult a trusted friend, family member, or colleague.

Sharing your experience can provide clarity and validation.

Ground Yourself in Facts

- Write down key details of events or conversations immediately after they occur. This record can help you stay grounded when the gaslighter attempts to rewrite history.

6. Use Observational Statements

When you suspect gaslighting in real-time, respond with observational statements that reflect what you notice without engaging in their distortions. This approach keeps you assertive and focused.

Examples:

- "That's not how I remember it, but I'm open to discussing it further."
- "It's interesting that you're saying this now, as it's different from what you said earlier."
- "I feel like my perspective is being dismissed. Let's revisit this later when we're both calm."

7. Create Emotional Distance

Gaslighting can feel overwhelming in the moment, but stepping back emotionally allows you to observe the situation more clearly.

Techniques:

- **Pause and Breathe:** Take a few deep breaths to calm yourself before responding.
- **Take a Time-Out:** Politely end the conversation and revisit it later if needed.
- **Detach Emotionally:** Remind yourself that their manipulative behavior reflects on them, not you.

Example: If someone says, "You're being too sensitive," respond with, "I need a moment to think about this," and disengage temporarily.

8. Practice Assertive Communication

Assertiveness can disrupt gaslighting attempts by showing that you trust your perspective and won't be easily manipulated.

Assertive Phrases:

- "I don't appreciate being made to feel like my concerns aren't valid."
- "I know what I experienced, and I'd like to discuss this calmly."
- "Let's focus on resolving the issue instead of assigning blame."

Being assertive doesn't mean being confrontational; it means standing firm in your truth while maintaining composure.

9. Seek Support and Validation

Gaslighting isolates victims, making them feel alone in their experiences. Counter this by seeking support from trusted individuals who can validate your reality.

Steps:

- Share specific examples of the behavior with a friend, therapist, or support group.
- Ask for their perspective to gain clarity and affirmation.
- Surround yourself with people who respect and validate your feelings.

10. Trust Your Instincts

Your instincts are a powerful tool for recognizing gaslighting. If something feels off, don't ignore it. Trusting your gut reaction can often help you identify manipulation before it takes root.

Ask Yourself:

- "Does this interaction feel supportive or dismissive?"
- "Am I walking away from this conversation feeling better or worse about myself?"

A Detailed Checklist of Gaslighting Red Flags

Gaslighting is a subtle form of psychological manipulation that can be challenging to identify, especially when it unfolds over time. By knowing the red flags, you can spot gaslighting behaviors early, protect your sense of reality, and take proactive steps to address the situation. Below is a detailed checklist of gaslighting red flags categorized into themes, with examples and insights into how each manifests in real life.

1. Denial and Distortion of Reality

Gaslighters often deny events or distort facts to create confusion and doubt.

- **Red Flags:**
    - They deny saying or doing something, even when you have clear evidence.
    Example: "I never said that; you're making it up."
    - They claim you're misremembering or imagining things.
    Example: "That's not how it happened at all."
    - They reinterpret past events to fit their narrative.
    Example: "You were the one who started the argument, not me."

2. Emotional Invalidation

Gaslighters dismiss or belittle your feelings, making you question their validity.

- **Red Flags:**
    - They accuse you of being overly emotional or sensitive.
    Example: "You're overreacting. It's not that big of a deal."

- They trivialize your concerns or experiences.
  Example: "Why are you upset about something so minor?"
- They make you feel guilty for expressing your emotions.
  Example: "You always take everything so personally."

3. Shifting Blame

Gaslighters avoid accountability by redirecting responsibility onto you or others.

- **Red Flags:**
  - They make you feel responsible for their actions or emotions.
    Example: "You made me do this by being so difficult."
  - They deflect criticism by focusing on your flaws or mistakes.
    Example: "You're accusing me? Look at all the things you've done wrong."
  - They turn the conversation into a critique of your behavior.
    Example: "This wouldn't be an issue if you weren't so stubborn."

4. Contradictory Statements

Gaslighters confuse you by frequently changing their story or perspective.

- **Red Flags:**
    - They contradict what they previously said without explanation.
      Example: "I never agreed to that," even though they clearly did.
    - They offer conflicting accounts of the same event.
      Example: "That's not what I meant earlier," despite having been clear.
    - They dismiss earlier statements by claiming you misunderstood.
      Example: "You must have taken what I said the wrong way."

5. Manipulation Through Guilt

Gaslighters exploit your sense of guilt to control or influence your behavior.

- **Red Flags:**
    - They accuse you of being selfish or ungrateful.
      Example: "After everything I've done for you, this is how you treat me?"
    - They frame themselves as the victim to gain sympathy.
      Example: "I'm always the one who gets blamed, no matter what."
    - They use your guilt to discourage you from asserting yourself.
      Example: "I guess I'm just a terrible person, according to you."

6. Isolation and Control

Gaslighters seek to isolate you from support systems to increase your dependency.

- **Red Flags:**
    - They discourage you from seeking advice or validation from others.
    Example: "You shouldn't talk to them about our issues—they'll only make things worse."
    - They create tension or conflict between you and your friends or family.
    Example: "Your friends don't really care about you like I do."
    - They insist they're the only person who truly understands or supports you.
    Example: "I'm the only one who has your best interests at heart."

7. Intermittent Affection and Criticism

Gaslighters alternate between kindness and manipulation to keep you emotionally invested.

- **Red Flags:**
    - They shower you with affection after being critical or dismissive.
    Example: "I know I can be hard on you, but I only do it because I love you."
    - They use small acts of kindness to make you doubt their harmful behavior.

Example: "See, I'm not that bad—I got you your favorite dessert."
- They switch between warm and cold behavior unpredictably.
Example: One day, they're supportive; the next, they're dismissive or hostile.

8. Making You Doubt Your Perception

Gaslighters intentionally sow doubt about your ability to perceive reality accurately.

- **Red Flags:**
    - They question your memory or judgment, making you second-guess yourself.
    **Example*:* "Are you sure you're remembering that correctly?"
    - They claim you're imagining things or being paranoid.
    Example: "You're just seeing things that aren't there."
    - They plant subtle suggestions to make you doubt your sanity.
    Example: "You've been really forgetful lately— are you feeling okay?"

9. Using Third Parties to Validate Their Narrative

Gaslighters involve others to reinforce their manipulative tactics.

- **Red Flags:**

- They claim others agree with their perspective, even if it's untrue.
  Example: "Everyone thinks you're being unreasonable."
- They enlist third parties to corroborate their version of events.
  Example: "Even your sister said you were out of line."
- They isolate you further by creating the impression that others are against you.
  Example: "No one else understands why you act this way, either."

10. Creating Dependence

Gaslighters work to make you reliant on them for validation and decision-making.

- **Red Flags:**
    - They undermine your confidence in making choices independently.
      Example: "You can't handle this on your own—you need me to help."
    - They make you feel incompetent or incapable.
      Example: "You wouldn't last a day without my support."
    - They position themselves as your sole source of truth or guidance.
      Example: "I'm the only one who really knows what's best for you."

11. Emotional Rollercoaster

Gaslighters thrive on creating instability in your emotions and self-esteem.

- **Red Flags:**
    - You feel confused, unsure, or emotionally drained after interactions with them.
    - Your mood and confidence fluctuate based on their behavior.
    - You often feel the need to justify yourself or seek their approval.

Using This Checklist

To use this checklist effectively:

1. **Observe Patterns:** Look for recurring behaviors rather than isolated incidents.
2. **Keep a Record:** Document specific interactions where these red flags appear.
3. **Trust Your Intuition:** If something feels off, it likely is—don't dismiss your instincts.
4. **Seek Support:** Share your observations with trusted friends, family, or a therapist for an external perspective.

The Emotional Barometer: A Tool for Tracking and Understanding Your Feelings

Gaslighting thrives on creating emotional confusion, self-doubt, and fear, making it difficult to trust your instincts and perceptions. The **Emotional Barometer** is a powerful exercise designed to help you monitor your emotional responses, recognize patterns, and identify when manipulation might be at play. By tracking your emotions, you can regain clarity and take steps to protect your mental well-being.

What Is the Emotional Barometer?

The Emotional Barometer is a self-awareness tool that helps you gauge and document your feelings in real-time or shortly after an interaction. Like a weather barometer measures atmospheric pressure, this exercise measures the "emotional pressure" you experience in your relationships, particularly during or after interactions with someone who might be gaslighting you.

Why Use the Emotional Barometer?

1. **Clarity:** It helps you identify patterns of emotional manipulation that may be hard to detect in the moment.
2. **Validation:** Documenting your feelings affirms your experiences, making it harder for someone to dismiss or distort them.
3. **Empowerment:** Understanding your emotional responses allows you to make informed decisions about how to address the situation.

How to Use the Emotional Barometer
Step 1: Set Up Your Barometer

Create a simple chart with the following columns:

1. **Date and Time**

2. **Interaction/Trigger**
3. **Primary Emotion(s)**
4. **Physical Reactions**
5. **Intensity Level**
6. **Possible Cause**
7. **Notes and Reflections**

Example Chart:

Date/Time	Interaction/Trigger	Primary Emotion(s)	Physical Reactions	Intensity Level (1-10)	Possible Cause	Notes and Reflections
12/07, 3 PM	Argument with Jamie	Confusion, Doubt	Tight chest, headache	8	Jamie denied our agreement about plans	Felt like I couldn't get my point across. Maybe I need to write things down to stay clear.

Step 2: Track Your Emotions

After each significant interaction or whenever you feel confused, self-doubting, or fearful, fill out the chart. Pay attention to the following elements:

- **Interaction/Trigger:**
  Briefly describe the situation or conversation that caused your emotional reaction.
    - **Example:** "Jamie said I misremembered a conversation we had last week."
- **Primary Emotion(s):**
  Identify the main emotions you experienced. Use descriptive terms like:
    - Confusion
    - Self-doubt
    - Fear
    - Guilt
    - Anxiety
- **Physical Reactions:**
  Note any physical sensations you experienced, as these are often tied to emotional distress:
    - Tightness in the chest
    - A sinking feeling in the stomach
    - Sweating or rapid heartbeat
- **Intensity Level (1-10):**
  Rate the emotional impact on a scale from 1 (mild) to 10 (overwhelming).
    - **Example:** "8 – I felt very disoriented and upset."
- **Possible Cause:**
  Reflect on what might have triggered your emotional response.

- **Example:** "Jamie's denial of our plans made me feel like I was losing my memory."
- **Notes and Reflections:**
Write down your observations, thoughts, or questions about the interaction. This step helps you process your emotions and identify patterns.
  - **Example:** "This isn't the first time Jamie has denied something we both agreed on. I feel like this might be a recurring pattern."

Step 3: Review and Reflect

At the end of each day or week, review your Emotional Barometer entries to identify recurring patterns or triggers. Look for:

- Specific interactions or individuals that consistently cause confusion, doubt, or fear.
- Emotional trends, such as a gradual increase in intensity over time.
- Physical symptoms that may indicate chronic stress or anxiety.

Sample Barometer Entry

Date/Time	Interaction/Trigger	Primary Emotion(s)	Physical Reactions	Intensity Level	Possible Cause	Notes and Reflections
12/07, 1 PM	Partner dismissed my	Doubt, Frustra	Tight chest, headac	7	Partner said, "You're	Feeling dismissed. This

Date/Time	Interaction/ Trigger	Primary Emotion(s)	Physical Reactions	Intensity Level	Possible Cause	Notes and Reflections
	feelings	tion	he		overreacting."	has happened before during conflicts.
12/08, 10 AM	Boss changed project instructions	Confusion, Anxiety	Racing thoughts, sweating	8	Boss claimed instructions were clear	I double-checked the email—it was vague. Documenting evidence helps.

Benefits of Using the Emotional Barometer

1. **Increased Awareness:**
   Tracking your emotions makes you more attuned to subtle manipulations.
2. **Validation of Experiences:**
   Seeing your feelings and reactions documented reinforces that your perceptions are real and important.

3. **Actionable Insights:**
   Identifying patterns empowers you to take steps to address gaslighting, such as setting boundaries or seeking support.
4. **Improved Emotional Regulation:**
   Reflecting on your responses helps you understand your triggers and manage your emotions effectively.

What to Do Next

Once you've tracked your emotions and identified potential gaslighting patterns:

1. **Seek Support:** Share your observations with a trusted friend, family member, or therapist.
2. **Establish Boundaries:** If someone consistently triggers negative emotions, consider setting clear boundaries to protect yourself.
3. **Document Interactions:** In cases where gaslighting involves work or legal matters, keeping a written record of interactions can be invaluable.
4. **Prioritize Self-Care:** Use relaxation techniques, such as deep breathing or mindfulness, to counteract the emotional toll of gaslighting.

Unique Analogies and Metaphors for Gaslighting Tactics

Gaslighting can be challenging to identify because it often operates subtly and under the radar. Using vivid analogies and metaphors can make these tactics easier to recognize and remember. Below are unique comparisons that illustrate common gaslighting behaviors, helping you understand their dynamics and impact.

1. "The Reality Twister" Effect

- **Metaphor:** Imagine being inside a funhouse where mirrors distort your reflection and the walls tilt at odd angles. What once felt stable and familiar now feels confusing and unreliable.
- **Explanation:** Gaslighters manipulate your perception of reality, much like a funhouse distorts your surroundings. They twist facts, deny events, and alter narratives, making you doubt what's real and what's imagined.
- **Example Behavior:** They deny having said something, even when you have evidence, leaving you feeling disoriented and questioning your memory.

2. "The Fog Machine" Tactic

- **Metaphor:** Picture walking through a dense fog where you can barely see a step ahead. You rely on someone to guide you, but they keep changing directions, adding to your disorientation.
- **Explanation:** Gaslighters create confusion by being vague, contradicting themselves, or withholding information. This "fog" makes you dependent on them for clarity, even though they're the ones causing your confusion.
- **Example Behavior:** They say, "You misunderstood me," or, "I already explained this to you," without providing clear answers.

3. "Emotional Erosion" Process

- **Metaphor:** Think of a steady drip of water eroding a rock over time. Individually, each drop seems harmless, but collectively, they wear down even the strongest stone.
- **Explanation:** Gaslighting doesn't always involve dramatic manipulations. Small, consistent invalidations and denials chip away at your confidence and sense of self over time.
- **Example Behavior:** Repeatedly dismissing your feelings with phrases like, "You're overreacting," or, "You're being too sensitive."

4. "The Puppet Master" Strategy

- **Metaphor:** Envision a puppet master pulling strings behind the scenes, controlling every move while convincing the puppet it's acting of its own free will.
- **Explanation:** Gaslighters manipulate you into behaving a certain way while making you believe it was your decision. They subtly influence your thoughts and actions to serve their agenda.
- **Example Behavior:** They suggest, "If I were you, I'd do this," planting ideas that align with their interests while making you think you came up with them.

5. "The Broken Compass" Technique

- **Metaphor:** Imagine relying on a compass that keeps pointing in random directions, making it impossible to

find your way. The more you try to follow it, the more lost you become.
- **Explanation:** Gaslighters act as your "compass," but they deliberately misguide you. They present themselves as a voice of reason while steering you further from the truth.
- **Example Behavior:** Claiming, "I'm just trying to help you see things clearly," while distorting the facts.

6. "The Mirror Maze" Game

- **Metaphor:** Picture yourself in a mirror maze, where reflections multiply and directions blur. Every time you think you've found the exit, you hit another glass wall.
- **Explanation:** Gaslighters use projection to reflect their faults onto you, making it hard to distinguish their actions from your own. You become trapped in their distorted version of reality.
- **Example Behavior:** Accusing you of being controlling or manipulative when they are the ones exhibiting those behaviors.

7. "The Pendulum Swing" Tactic

- **Metaphor:** Visualize a pendulum swinging between extremes, never settling in one place. One moment it's calm and steady; the next, it's chaotic and erratic.
- **Explanation:** Gaslighters alternate between kindness and criticism, keeping you emotionally off-balance and unsure of where you stand.

- **Example Behavior:** Praising you one day for your intelligence, then belittling you the next for making a simple mistake.

8. "The Illusionist's Trick"

- **Metaphor:** Imagine a magician distracting you with one hand while performing a trick with the other. By the time you realize what's happened, the illusion is complete.
- **Explanation:** Gaslighters use diversion tactics to shift focus away from their behavior and onto yours. They create distractions to keep you from addressing the real issue.
- **Example Behavior:** When confronted about their actions, they respond with, "Why are you always so critical of me?"

9. "The Sandcastle Effect"

- **Metaphor:** Picture building a sandcastle near the shoreline, only for the waves to wash away your progress. No matter how hard you try, it feels impossible to build something that lasts.
- **Explanation:** Gaslighters undermine your self-esteem and confidence, making it hard to maintain a stable sense of self. Every time you feel secure, they erode it with criticism or doubt.
- **Example Behavior:** Saying, "You're not as capable as you think," after you express pride in an accomplishment.

10. "The Chameleon Approach"

- **Metaphor:** Think of a chameleon blending seamlessly into its surroundings, adapting its appearance to fit the environment.
- **Explanation:** Gaslighters change their behavior, tone, or stance depending on the situation to manipulate you more effectively. They can be charming and supportive in public but dismissive and critical in private.
- **Example Behavior:** Acting loving and supportive around others but invalidating your feelings when you're alone.

11. "The Domino Effect" Manipulation

- **Metaphor:** Imagine a single push setting off a chain reaction that topples every domino in a carefully arranged line.
- **Explanation:** Gaslighters use one manipulative act to trigger a cascade of self-doubt, guilt, and confusion. Their actions are calculated to create ripple effects that destabilize you.
- **Example Behavior:** Saying, "If you cared about me, you wouldn't doubt me," leading you to question your feelings, actions, and intentions.

12. "The Echo Chamber" Dynamic

- **Metaphor:** Picture yourself in a room where every sound you make is repeated back to you, distorted and amplified.

- **Explanation:** Gaslighters echo your concerns or criticisms back at you but twist them to serve their narrative. This creates confusion and deflects attention from their behavior.
- **Example Behavior:** When you say, "I feel like you're not listening to me," they respond with, "No, you're the one who never listens."

How to Use These Analogies

1. **Recognize the Pattern:** These metaphors serve as a mental shortcut to identify gaslighting tactics when they occur.
2. **Name the Behavior:** Use the analogy to label what's happening. For example, "This feels like the Fog Machine—things are intentionally unclear."
3. **Stay Grounded:** Analogies can help you detach emotionally and observe the behavior objectively.
4. **Take Action:** Once you've identified the tactic, use assertive communication or boundaries to address it.

Chapter 4: The Impact of Gaslighting on Your Mental Health

Gaslighting is not just a manipulation tactic; it's an emotionally and psychologically destructive experience. Its effects can ripple through your mental health, leaving long-lasting scars that are often invisible to others but deeply felt by those who endure it. This chapter explores the profound impact gaslighting has on your mental and emotional well-being, helping you recognize its toll and take the first steps toward recovery.

1. Erosion of Self-Esteem

Gaslighting systematically undermines your confidence and sense of self-worth.

- **How It Happens:**
    - Constant invalidation of your feelings makes you question your emotional responses.
    - Repeated denial of your experiences creates self-doubt about your memory and perceptions.
    - Manipulative comparisons or critiques erode your belief in your abilities.
- **Impact:**
    - You may feel incompetent, inadequate, or overly dependent on others for validation.
    - Over time, you begin to internalize the gaslighter's negative narrative about you.

Example: You start second-guessing your decisions, even in unrelated areas of your life, because you've been made to feel incapable of making good choices.

2. Chronic Anxiety and Fear

Gaslighting creates an atmosphere of unpredictability that fosters constant anxiety.

- **How It Happens:**
    - The gaslighter's behavior is inconsistent, alternating between affection and criticism.
    - You're often walking on eggshells, fearing their reaction or another confrontation.
    - The uncertainty of whether your perspective will be validated keeps you in a state of hypervigilance.
- **Impact:**
    - You may experience symptoms of anxiety, such as racing thoughts, difficulty concentrating, or physical tension.
    - Everyday decisions or interactions become sources of stress, as you worry about how they'll be perceived.

Example: You avoid expressing your opinions or needs, fearing backlash or dismissal.

3. Depression and Hopelessness

Over time, the emotional toll of gaslighting can lead to feelings of despair and helplessness.

- **How It Happens:**
    - Gaslighters isolate you from support systems, making you feel alone and misunderstood.
    - They invalidate your experiences, leading you to question whether your struggles are even real.
    - The ongoing cycle of manipulation can make it seem like there's no escape.
- **Impact:**
    - Symptoms of depression, such as fatigue, sadness, and a lack of motivation, may emerge.
    - You may feel stuck, believing that no one will believe or support you if you try to leave the situation.

Example: You start to believe that things will never change and feel powerless to improve your circumstances.

4. Identity Confusion

Gaslighting disrupts your sense of self, leaving you unsure of who you are and what you stand for.

- **How It Happens:**
    - The gaslighter questions your memories, preferences, and values, creating doubt about your identity.
    - You begin to prioritize their perspective over your own, losing touch with your instincts and desires.
    - Repeated invalidation leads to a fragmented sense of self.
- **Impact:**

- You may struggle to articulate your thoughts or make decisions without second-guessing yourself.
- The loss of self-trust can make it difficult to set boundaries or advocate for your needs.

Example: You find yourself agreeing with others to avoid conflict, even when their views don't align with your true beliefs.

5. Cognitive Dissonance

Gaslighting forces you to reconcile conflicting realities, creating mental and emotional strain.

- **How It Happens:**
    - The gaslighter's words and actions don't align, leaving you confused about their intentions.
    - They create a distorted version of events that conflicts with your memory or understanding.
    - You begin to doubt your own perception in an attempt to reduce the discomfort of conflicting beliefs.
- **Impact:**
    - This constant mental tug-of-war can lead to mental exhaustion and difficulty processing information.
    - Over time, you may default to accepting the gaslighter's narrative to avoid further confusion.

Example: You start to believe their version of events, even when it contradicts your instincts, because it feels easier than constantly questioning yourself.

6. Isolation and Loneliness

Gaslighters often alienate their victims from support networks, leaving them feeling alone and misunderstood.

- **How It Happens:**
    - They discredit your relationships, suggesting that friends or family members are unreliable or unsupportive.
    - They create tension or conflict between you and your loved ones, further isolating you.
    - Their constant invalidation makes you hesitant to share your experiences with others.
- **Impact:**
    - The lack of external validation exacerbates your self-doubt and reliance on the gaslighter.
    - Loneliness can deepen feelings of depression and hopelessness.

Example: You stop reaching out to friends, believing the gaslighter's claim that "no one else understands you like I do."

7. Trauma and PTSD Symptoms

In severe cases, prolonged gaslighting can lead to trauma or post-traumatic stress disorder (PTSD).

- **How It Happens:**

- The constant manipulation and invalidation create an ongoing sense of danger or instability.
- Emotional abuse triggers a fight-or-flight response that can persist long after the gaslighting ends.
- Memories of the manipulation may resurface as intrusive thoughts or flashbacks.
- **Impact:**
  - You may experience hypervigilance, emotional numbness, or difficulty trusting others.
  - Triggers, such as certain phrases or behaviors, may evoke intense emotional reactions.

Example: Hearing someone dismiss your feelings reminds you of the gaslighter's behavior, causing anxiety or distress.

8. Self-Isolation and Withdrawal

The emotional exhaustion caused by gaslighting can lead you to withdraw from others and from life.

- **How It Happens:**
  - You fear being misunderstood or invalidated by others, so you avoid social interactions.
  - The mental effort of constantly defending your reality feels overwhelming, leading you to retreat.
  - The gaslighter's influence makes you question whether your feelings are worth sharing.
- **Impact:**
  - Isolation deepens your dependence on the gaslighter and reinforces their control.

- Withdrawal from activities and relationships contributes to feelings of loneliness and despair.

Example: You cancel plans with friends, believing that your concerns will only burden them.

Steps to Recognize and Address the Impact

Recognizing the mental health toll of gaslighting is the first step toward healing. Here's how to begin:

1. **Acknowledge Your Feelings:**
   Validate your emotions, even if the gaslighter has dismissed them. Your feelings are real and important.
2. **Seek Support:**
   Reach out to trusted friends, family, or a therapist to share your experiences and gain perspective.
3. **Document Interactions:**
   Keeping a journal can help you track patterns of gaslighting and affirm your reality.
4. **Set Boundaries:**
   Limit your exposure to the gaslighter and prioritize relationships that nurture your mental health.
5. **Practice Self-Compassion:**
   Remind yourself that gaslighting is not your fault and that healing takes time.

The Psychological Toll of Gaslighting: Trauma, Anxiety, and Self-Esteem Issues

Gaslighting is a deeply insidious form of psychological manipulation that not only erodes trust in others but also damages the victim's relationship with themselves. Its effects ripple across various aspects of mental health, creating a toxic cycle of trauma, anxiety, and diminished self-esteem. In this expert-backed discussion, we delve into the psychological mechanisms behind these issues, providing insights into their causes, manifestations, and paths to recovery.

1. Gaslighting and Trauma: A Silent Psychological Wound
Understanding Trauma in the Context of Gaslighting

Trauma isn't limited to physical harm or catastrophic events; psychological abuse like gaslighting can also lead to trauma. Gaslighting is uniquely damaging because it distorts the victim's reality, creating a sense of instability and emotional harm that mirrors the effects of other forms of abuse.

- **Key Characteristics of Trauma from Gaslighting:**
    - Persistent feelings of confusion, betrayal, and fear.
    - Difficulty trusting others or even oneself.
    - Hypervigilance to avoid further manipulation or harm.

How Gaslighting Creates Trauma

According to trauma experts like Dr. Judith Herman (*Trauma and Recovery*), psychological trauma occurs when an individual's sense of safety, trust, and control is violated. Gaslighting achieves this by:

- **Disrupting Reality:** Victims are forced to question their memories, perceptions, and beliefs.
- **Eroding Trust:** The manipulator's denial and distortion of facts create a profound sense of betrayal.
- **Inducing Helplessness:** Over time, victims feel powerless to resist or escape the manipulation.

Symptoms of Gaslighting-Induced Trauma

- Flashbacks or intrusive thoughts about the manipulation.
- Emotional numbness or detachment as a coping mechanism.
- Avoidance of situations or relationships that trigger memories of gaslighting.

2. Anxiety: The Lingering Effect of Constant Doubt

Understanding Anxiety in Gaslighting Victims

Gaslighting thrives on creating uncertainty, leaving victims in a perpetual state of self-doubt. This constant questioning of one's reality can lead to chronic anxiety, a mental health condition characterized by excessive worry and fear.

- **How Gaslighting Leads to Anxiety:**
    - **Hypervigilance:** Victims become overly cautious in interactions, fearing further manipulation or invalidation.
    - **Fear of Conflict:** Gaslighters often escalate situations when confronted, leading victims to avoid expressing concerns or asserting boundaries.

- **Uncertainty and Doubt:** Repeated denials and distortions create a fear of being wrong or misunderstood.

Manifestations of Anxiety

Victims of gaslighting may experience:

- **Physical Symptoms:** Racing heart, sweating, headaches, or stomach issues.
- **Cognitive Symptoms:** Difficulty concentrating, overthinking, or indecisiveness.
- **Behavioral Symptoms:** Avoidance of social interactions, reluctance to make decisions, or excessive reassurance-seeking.

Expert Perspective

Dr. Bessel van der Kolk, author of *The Body Keeps the Score*, emphasizes that anxiety is often the body's response to unresolved emotional stress. For gaslighting victims, the constant manipulation triggers the body's fight-or-flight response, creating a cycle of stress and fear.

3. Self-Esteem: The Erosion of Confidence
How Gaslighting Destroys Self-Esteem

Gaslighting is a direct attack on a person's confidence and sense of self-worth. By invalidating their thoughts, feelings, and experiences, gaslighters erode the victim's ability to trust their instincts, leading to a fractured sense of identity.

- **Common Tactics That Harm Self-Esteem:**
  - **Emotional Invalidation:** Dismissing the victim's feelings as irrational or exaggerated.
  - **Criticism Disguised as Help:** "I'm only saying this because I care about you" is often used to mask belittling remarks.
  - **Comparison and Triangulation:** Pitting the victim against others to make them feel inadequate.

Signs of Low Self-Esteem in Gaslighting Victims

- Reluctance to express opinions or assert needs.
- Excessive self-blame or apologizing for things outside their control.
- Difficulty making decisions without seeking external validation.

The Long-Term Impact

Low self-esteem doesn't just affect relationships—it seeps into all areas of life. Victims may struggle with career growth, avoid new opportunities, or stay in toxic situations because they don't believe they deserve better.

Expert Insights

Psychologist Dr. Kristin Neff, a leading researcher in self-compassion, highlights that individuals with low self-esteem often lack self-compassion. Gaslighting victims internalize criticism and blame, making it harder to view themselves with kindness or understanding.

Breaking Free: Addressing the Psychological Toll

Recovering from the trauma, anxiety, and self-esteem issues caused by gaslighting is possible, but it requires intentional effort and support. Below are strategies recommended by mental health experts:

1. Rebuilding Trust in Yourself

- **Practice Reality Checks:** Document events and conversations to validate your memory and experiences.
- **Challenge Negative Thoughts:** Replace self-doubt with affirmations like, "My feelings are valid" or "I deserve to be heard."

2. Managing Anxiety

- **Mindfulness Practices:** Techniques like deep breathing, meditation, or grounding exercises can reduce anxiety and help you stay present.
- **Set Boundaries:** Limit exposure to gaslighters and prioritize relationships that nurture your mental health.

3. Restoring Self-Esteem

- **Self-Compassion Exercises:** Dr. Neff's self-compassion framework encourages treating yourself with the same kindness you'd offer a friend.
- **Therapy:** Cognitive-behavioral therapy (CBT) and trauma-focused therapy can help rebuild confidence and address underlying issues.

4. Seeking Support

- **Therapists and Counselors:** Professionals can provide tools and techniques tailored to your needs.
- **Support Groups:** Connecting with others who've experienced gaslighting can offer validation and encouragement.
- **Trusted Allies:** Share your journey with friends or family who respect and uplift you.

Stories of Resilience and Recovery: Gaslighting Survivors Reclaim Their Lives

Gaslighting can leave victims feeling broken, confused, and powerless. However, recovery is not only possible but often leads to profound personal growth and resilience. The stories below, while fictionalized for privacy, are inspired by the real experiences of survivors who have reclaimed their lives and rebuilt their confidence after enduring the trauma of gaslighting. These narratives highlight the courage it takes to confront manipulation and the steps individuals have taken to heal and thrive.

1. Emily: Rebuilding Confidence After Workplace Gaslighting
The Challenge

Emily, a 35-year-old marketing professional, worked under a manager who consistently undermined her abilities. Despite her innovative ideas and strong performance, her manager frequently took credit for her work and dismissed her concerns with phrases like, "You're overthinking things," or, "You're not ready for a leadership role."

Over time, Emily began to doubt her skills and capabilities. She hesitated to voice her ideas in meetings and started second-guessing her decisions, fearing criticism or dismissal.

The Turning Point

After a particularly stressful project where her manager blatantly denied prior agreements, Emily confided in a trusted colleague. The colleague validated her experiences and encouraged her to document interactions and seek mentorship outside her immediate team.

The Recovery

Emily took several proactive steps to rebuild her confidence:

- **Documentation:** She began keeping detailed records of her work and interactions with her manager. This not only provided clarity but also empowered her to challenge false claims.
- **External Validation:** She joined a professional networking group where she received constructive feedback and support from peers.
- **Advocating for Herself:** Armed with evidence, Emily eventually approached HR, leading to a resolution and transfer to a more supportive team.

The Outcome

Today, Emily is thriving in a senior marketing role. She credits her recovery to the support of colleagues and her decision to prioritize her mental well-being. Reflecting on her experience, she says, "Gaslighting made me question everything, but I learned that my voice matters. Now, I never hesitate to stand up for myself."

2. David: Breaking Free from a Manipulative Friendship
The Challenge

David, a 29-year-old software engineer, had been close friends with Mark since college. Over time, Mark's behavior became increasingly manipulative. He would make subtle jabs at David's choices, saying things like, "Are you sure you're cut out for that job?" or, "Your other friends aren't really there for you like I am."

Whenever David tried to address these comments, Mark would deflect, saying, "You're being too sensitive," or, "I'm just looking out for you." David felt trapped, doubting his instincts but fearing the loss of a long-standing friendship.

The Turning Point

After confiding in his sister, David realized that Mark's behavior had left him feeling drained and isolated. His sister helped him see the pattern of manipulation and encouraged him to seek therapy to gain clarity.

The Recovery

David's path to recovery involved several key steps:

- **Therapy:** Working with a therapist, David unpacked the dynamics of the friendship and recognized how Mark's comments had eroded his self-esteem.
- **Setting Boundaries:** David began limiting his interactions with Mark, refusing to engage in conversations that felt dismissive or critical.
- **Building New Connections:** He made an effort to reconnect with old friends and join new social groups, creating a more supportive network.

The Outcome

David eventually ended the friendship, a decision that felt liberating rather than regretful. "Letting go of Mark was hard," David shares, "but I realized I deserve relationships that uplift me. Now, I feel more confident and grounded than ever."

3. Sofia: Rediscovering Herself After an Abusive Relationship
The Challenge

Sofia, a 42-year-old teacher, had been in a 10-year marriage with a partner who used gaslighting to control her. Her husband would deny hurtful comments, rewrite events to blame her, and isolate her from friends and family, saying things like, "They're just jealous of our relationship."

Over time, Sofia felt like a shadow of her former self. She doubted her memories, avoided conflict, and became emotionally dependent on her husband.

The Turning Point

One evening, after a particularly heated argument where her husband accused her of being "too dramatic," Sofia confided in her best friend. Her friend shared similar stories of emotional abuse from others and urged Sofia to seek help.

The Recovery

Sofia's journey to recovery was gradual but transformative:

- **Seeking Professional Help:** Sofia began therapy, where she learned to recognize gaslighting patterns and rebuild her sense of self-worth.
- **Journaling:** Writing about her experiences helped her process emotions and regain trust in her memories.
- **Support Groups:** Joining a group for survivors of emotional abuse provided Sofia with validation and a sense of community.

The Outcome

Sofia eventually left the marriage and started a new chapter in her life. She now mentors other survivors, sharing her story to inspire hope. "I thought I'd lost myself," Sofia reflects, "but leaving that relationship helped me find a stronger, braver version of me."

4. Liam: Overcoming Family Gaslighting
The Challenge

Liam, a 25-year-old college student, grew up in a family where his parents often dismissed his feelings and belittled his achievements. When he expressed frustration or sadness, they'd respond with comments like, "You're just being dramatic," or, "You should be grateful for what you have."

These interactions left Liam feeling invalidated and confused about his emotions. He began suppressing his feelings, fearing they weren't justified or worth sharing.

The Turning Point

In a psychology class, Liam learned about gaslighting and realized his parents' behavior matched many of the patterns described. This awareness was a pivotal moment, helping him see that his feelings were valid and his experiences were real.

The Recovery

Liam took steps to reclaim his emotional health:

- **Education:** He read books on emotional abuse and gaslighting, gaining tools to navigate his family dynamics.
- **Setting Emotional Boundaries:** Liam limited how much he shared with his parents and focused on cultivating relationships with supportive friends and mentors.

- **Practicing Self-Validation:** He started affirming his feelings and decisions, building confidence in his judgment.

The Outcome

Today, Liam has a healthier perspective on his family relationships. "I still love my parents," Liam explains, "but I've learned to protect my peace and surround myself with people who value me for who I am."

Lessons from These Stories

1. **Awareness Is the First Step:** Recognizing gaslighting patterns is crucial for breaking free from manipulation.
2. **Support Systems Matter:** Whether it's friends, family, or professionals, having a support network can make all the difference.
3. **Healing Takes Time:** Recovery from gaslighting is a gradual process that requires patience and self-compassion.
4. **Resilience Is Possible:** These stories show that, despite the damage gaslighting can cause, it is possible to rebuild confidence, trust, and a fulfilling life.

Actionable Tips to Begin Healing While Experiencing Gaslighting

Healing from gaslighting can feel impossible when you're still in the midst of manipulation, but taking small, actionable steps can help you regain clarity, build resilience, and reclaim your sense of self. Below are detailed strategies you can use to start the healing process even while navigating ongoing gaslighting.

1. Name the Behavior: Recognize It for What It Is

The first step to healing is identifying and naming gaslighting when it occurs. Awareness is empowering and helps you detach emotionally from the manipulative behavior.

- **What to Do:**
    - Keep a journal to document specific instances of gaslighting. Write down what was said, how you felt, and why it felt manipulative.
    - Use terms like "emotional invalidation" or "reality distortion" to label the gaslighter's tactics.
- **Why It Works:**
    - Naming the behavior removes some of its power and helps you see it as a tactic rather than a reflection of your reality.

Example: When someone says, "You're just being dramatic," mentally note, *This is emotional invalidation, not a reflection of my feelings.*

2. Ground Yourself in Reality

Gaslighting thrives on creating confusion and self-doubt. Grounding techniques can help you stay connected to your perceptions and memories.

- **What to Do:**

- **Document Events:** Write down key conversations, agreements, or incidents immediately after they happen. This creates a reference point for when the gaslighter denies or distorts them.
- **Use Visual Cues:** Keep physical evidence of agreements or actions, such as emails, text messages, or receipts, to validate your reality.
- **Affirm Your Experiences:** Regularly remind yourself, "My feelings and perceptions are valid."
- **Why It Works:**
  - Grounding techniques provide clarity and reduce the gaslighter's ability to manipulate your perception of events.

Example: When the gaslighter denies a previous agreement, refer to your notes or messages for confirmation.

3. Build a Support Network

Gaslighting often isolates victims, making them feel alone and dependent on the manipulator. Connecting with supportive people is crucial to counteract this.

- **What to Do:**
  - Reach out to trusted friends, family members, or colleagues who validate your feelings and experiences.
  - Share specific examples of the gaslighting behavior to help them understand your situation.
  - Consider joining a support group for survivors of emotional abuse.

- **Why It Works:**
    - Supportive relationships provide external validation, helping you trust your perceptions and rebuild confidence.

Example: Share a troubling interaction with a trusted friend and ask, "Does this sound like gaslighting to you?"

4. Set Boundaries to Protect Your Emotional Energy

Even while experiencing gaslighting, you can set boundaries to limit its impact on your mental health.

- **What to Do:**
    - **Limit Engagement:** Minimize time spent with the gaslighter or redirect conversations when they become manipulative.
    - **Practice Assertiveness:** Use clear, firm language to set boundaries. For example, "I don't appreciate being dismissed. Let's revisit this later."
    - **Emotional Detachment:** Visualize a "shield" around yourself to protect against harmful words or actions.
- **Why It Works:**
    - Boundaries reduce your exposure to manipulation and signal to the gaslighter that you're not easily controlled.

Example: If a gaslighter tries to escalate a conflict, say, "I need time to process this. Let's discuss it another time."

5. Focus on Self-Care and Stress Reduction

Gaslighting takes a toll on your mental and physical health. Prioritizing self-care helps you build resilience and cope with stress.

- **What to Do:**
    - **Practice Relaxation Techniques:** Use deep breathing, meditation, or yoga to calm your mind and body.
    - **Engage in Activities You Enjoy:** Dedicate time to hobbies or interests that bring you joy and distract you from the manipulation.
    - **Exercise Regularly:** Physical activity releases endorphins, reducing stress and improving mood.
- **Why It Works:**
    - Self-care restores balance, boosts emotional strength, and reduces the immediate impact of gaslighting.

Example: After a difficult interaction, take a walk, listen to calming music, or engage in a creative activity.

6. Reconnect with Your Inner Voice

Gaslighting disconnects you from your instincts and self-trust. Rebuilding that connection is a critical part of healing.

- **What to Do:**
    - **Journaling:** Reflect on your thoughts and feelings daily to process your experiences and affirm your reality.

- **Practice Self-Validation:** Replace self-doubt with affirmations like, "I trust my instincts," or, "My emotions are valid."
- **Trust Small Decisions:** Rebuild confidence by making and trusting small choices, like what to eat or wear.
- **Why It Works:**
  - Reconnecting with your inner voice helps you regain trust in your judgment and reinforces your autonomy.

Example: When the gaslighter questions your memory, tell yourself, "I know what I remember, and that's enough."

7. Educate Yourself About Gaslighting

Understanding gaslighting and its effects can empower you to recognize and resist manipulation.

- **What to Do:**
  - Read books, articles, or watch videos about gaslighting and emotional abuse.
  - Learn about common gaslighting tactics, such as denial, projection, and blame-shifting.
  - Explore resources on building emotional resilience and setting boundaries.
- **Why It Works:**
  - Knowledge is power. Understanding gaslighting gives you tools to protect yourself and regain control.

Example: Recognizing that a gaslighter's criticism is a projection of their insecurities can help you detach emotionally.

8. Seek Professional Support

Therapists and counselors can provide invaluable guidance for navigating and recovering from gaslighting.

- **What to Do:**
    - Look for a therapist who specializes in emotional abuse or trauma recovery.
    - Explore cognitive-behavioral therapy (CBT) to address self-doubt and build coping strategies.
    - Consider group therapy to connect with others facing similar challenges.
- **Why It Works:**
    - Professional support provides a safe space to process your emotions and develop personalized strategies for healing.

Example: A therapist can help you identify recurring gaslighting patterns and develop specific responses to address them.

9. Develop a Long-Term Exit Strategy

If possible, plan for a future where you are no longer exposed to the gaslighter's behavior.

- **What to Do:**

- Identify steps you can take to reduce dependence on the gaslighter, such as securing financial independence or building alternative support networks.
- Outline actionable goals for distancing yourself from the manipulative relationship.
- Seek legal or professional advice if the gaslighting occurs in a workplace or involves other forms of abuse.
- **Why It Works:**
    - Knowing you have a plan for eventual freedom provides hope and motivation to endure and heal in the meantime.

Example: Begin saving money or seeking alternative employment to create a pathway out of a toxic work environment.

10. Celebrate Small Victories

Every step you take to reclaim your sense of self, no matter how small, is a victory worth celebrating.

- **What to Do:**
    - Acknowledge progress, such as recognizing gaslighting patterns or setting a boundary.
    - Reward yourself for taking positive steps, like journaling or reaching out to a friend.
    - Reflect on your resilience and growth, even amid challenges.
- **Why It Works:**

- Celebrating small victories builds momentum and reinforces your belief in your ability to overcome the effects of gaslighting.

Example: After successfully standing your ground in an argument, treat yourself to something you enjoy, like a favorite meal or a relaxing activity.

Chapter 5: Breaking the Cycle: Setting Boundaries and Saying No

Gaslighting thrives in an environment where boundaries are blurred, and saying "no" feels like a confrontation rather than an assertion of your autonomy. Breaking free from this cycle requires a conscious effort to reclaim your personal power by setting clear boundaries and learning to say no with confidence. In this chapter, we'll explore actionable steps to stand up to gaslighters, maintain your sense of self, and cultivate healthier relationships.

1. The Importance of Boundaries

Boundaries are the invisible lines that define what behavior you will and won't accept in your relationships. They protect your emotional well-being and help you maintain a sense of autonomy.

- **Why Boundaries Matter:**
    - They create clarity in relationships by defining acceptable behavior.
    - They empower you to take control of your interactions and protect your mental health.
    - They signal to gaslighters that their manipulative tactics will no longer work.

Example: A boundary might look like saying, "I won't continue this conversation if my feelings are being dismissed."

2. Recognizing Your Right to Say No

Gaslighters often rely on guilt, fear, or manipulation to make you feel obligated to comply with their demands. Recognizing that you have the right to say no is a critical step toward breaking free.

- **Reframing "No":**
    - Understand that saying no is not selfish or unkind—it's a way of honoring your needs.
    - Realize that you don't owe anyone an explanation for protecting your boundaries.

Example: Instead of feeling pressured to explain your decision, say, "No, that doesn't work for me," and leave it at that.

3. Identify Your Personal Boundaries

Before you can set boundaries, you need to identify your limits and values.

- **How to Define Your Boundaries:**
    - Reflect on past interactions where you felt uncomfortable, dismissed, or manipulated. What behaviors crossed the line for you?
    - Ask yourself what you need to feel respected and valued in your relationships.
    - Consider your non-negotiables—actions or words you will not tolerate under any circumstances.

Example: If a gaslighter frequently invalidates your feelings, a boundary might be, "I won't engage in conversations where my emotions are dismissed."

4. Communicating Boundaries Effectively

Gaslighters often test boundaries to maintain control. Communicating your limits clearly and assertively is essential to enforcing them.

- **Steps to Communicate Boundaries:**
    - **Be Direct:** Use concise and firm language.
      Example: "Please don't criticize my choices. I've made my decision."
    - **State Consequences:** Let them know what will happen if the boundary is crossed.
      Example: "If you continue to dismiss my feelings, I'll end the conversation."
    - **Stay Calm:** Avoid becoming defensive or emotional, as this can fuel the gaslighter's tactics.

Script for Saying No:

- "I understand your perspective, but I'm not comfortable with that."
- "That's not something I'm willing to do."
- "No, thank you. I've made up my mind."

5. Anticipate Pushback and Manipulative Tactics

Gaslighters are likely to resist your boundaries and test your resolve. Knowing how to handle their pushback is crucial to maintaining your autonomy.

- **Common Gaslighter Responses:**
    - **Guilt Trips:** "After everything I've done for you, you're really going to say no?"
    - **Deflection:** "Why are you being so difficult? This isn't a big deal."
    - **Victimhood:** "You're hurting me by not agreeing."
- **How to Respond:**
    - Repeat your boundary without engaging in their narrative.
      Example: "I hear what you're saying, but my decision remains the same."
    - Use the "broken record" technique: calmly repeat your boundary until they stop pushing.

6. Enforcing Consequences

Setting boundaries is only effective if you're willing to enforce them. Gaslighters will often test your limits to see if they can push past them.

- **How to Enforce Boundaries:**
    - Follow through on the consequences you stated.
      Example: If you said you'd leave the conversation, do so if the boundary is crossed.

- Limit or end interactions with the gaslighter if they repeatedly violate your boundaries.
- Seek support if necessary, whether through friends, family, or a professional.

Example: If a gaslighter continues to invalidate your feelings, say, "I won't continue this conversation. Let's revisit it later if we can approach it respectfully," and walk away.

7. Practice Self-Affirmation

Gaslighting can erode your confidence, making it difficult to stand firm in your boundaries. Practicing self-affirmation helps rebuild your self-trust and resilience.

- **Affirmations to Repeat:**
    - "My boundaries are valid and deserve to be respected."
    - "I have the right to protect my emotional well-being."
    - "Saying no is an act of self-care, not selfishness."

Example: Before a challenging interaction, remind yourself, "I am in control of my choices, and I won't let manipulation sway me."

8. Seek Support and Validation

Breaking free from gaslighting is easier with a strong support system. Surround yourself with people who validate and respect your boundaries.

- **How to Build Support:**
    - Share your experiences with trusted friends or family members.
    - Join support groups for survivors of gaslighting or emotional abuse.
    - Work with a therapist to develop strategies for setting and enforcing boundaries.

Example: After a difficult interaction, debrief with a supportive friend who can affirm your decision to stand firm.

9. Focus on Building Healthy Relationships

As you enforce boundaries with gaslighters, prioritize relationships that are supportive and respectful.

- **Traits of Healthy Relationships:**
    - Mutual respect for boundaries and autonomy.
    - Open communication and willingness to listen.
    - Supportive behavior that fosters trust and emotional safety.

Example: Cultivate friendships where your feelings are validated, and your boundaries are seen as an expression of self-care, not conflict.

10. Reflect and Adjust

Setting boundaries is an ongoing process that requires reflection and adjustment. As you gain confidence, you may find the need to expand or refine your limits.

- **Questions for Reflection:**
  - Which boundaries have been effective?
  - Are there areas where I need to set stronger limits?
  - How have I grown in asserting myself since I started this journey?

Example: After successfully enforcing a boundary, reflect on how it made you feel and consider how you can apply this confidence to other areas of your life.

Scripts for Responding to Common Gaslighting Scenarios

Gaslighting thrives on manipulation, confusion, and invalidation. Having prepared responses—or "scripts"—for common gaslighting scenarios can help you stay calm, assertive, and focused on your truth. Below are detailed scripts tailored to specific contexts, such as workplace interactions, romantic relationships, and family dynamics, empowering you to respond effectively to gaslighting in real-time.

1. Workplace Gaslighting

Gaslighting in the workplace often involves undermining your credibility, shifting blame, or rewriting history. These scripts are designed to help you maintain professionalism while addressing the behavior.

Scenario 1: Denial of Agreements

Situation: Your manager denies giving specific instructions for a project, leaving you feeling confused and responsible for their oversight.

Script:

- "I remember discussing this during our meeting on [date]. Let me pull up my notes to clarify what was agreed upon."
- "To ensure we're aligned moving forward, I'd like to summarize our discussions in writing after meetings. This will help us avoid any misunderstandings."

Why It Works:
Referring to documented evidence shifts the focus back to the facts, minimizing the gaslighter's ability to distort reality.

Scenario 2: Undermining Your Work

Situation: A coworker takes credit for your idea or diminishes your contributions in a meeting.

Script:

- "I'm glad you liked the idea I brought up last week. Let's build on it together to move the project forward."
- "I'd like to revisit the original concept I shared to ensure we're giving proper credit to all contributions."

Why It Works:
This response assertively reclaims ownership of your work

without appearing confrontational, reinforcing your role in the discussion.

2. Romantic Relationship Gaslighting

In romantic relationships, gaslighting often involves emotional invalidation, blame-shifting, or rewriting past events. These scripts help you set boundaries and address manipulative behavior.

Scenario 1: Emotional Invalidation

Situation: Your partner dismisses your feelings, saying, "You're overreacting. It's not a big deal."

Script:

- "My feelings are valid, even if you don't see it that way. I'd like us to focus on understanding each other rather than dismissing emotions."
- "I feel hurt when my emotions are minimized. Can we work on addressing the issue together instead of focusing on how I should feel?"

Why It Works:
This response affirms your emotions and shifts the conversation toward collaborative problem-solving.

Scenario 2: Blame-Shifting

Situation: Your partner blames you for their actions, saying, "If you hadn't done that, I wouldn't have reacted this way."

Script:

- "I can understand how my actions may have affected you, but your response is still your responsibility. Let's talk about how we can both handle this better in the future."
- "I'm open to discussing how we can improve our communication, but I won't take responsibility for actions that weren't mine."

Why It Works:
This response acknowledges their feelings while firmly rejecting blame for their behavior.

3. Family Dynamics Gaslighting

Gaslighting in family settings often involves guilt-tripping, rewriting family history, or dismissing boundaries. These scripts provide tools to address manipulation while maintaining composure.

Scenario 1: Rewriting History

Situation: A parent denies ever making a hurtful comment, saying, "I never said that. You're imagining things."

Script:

- "I remember the conversation differently, and it's important for me to acknowledge how it made me feel. Let's focus on moving forward from here."

- "Whether it was intentional or not, what was said hurt me. I'd like us to discuss how we can communicate better in the future."

Why It Works:
This response validates your experience while steering the conversation toward constructive dialogue.

Scenario 2: Guilt-Tripping

Situation: A family member says, "After everything I've done for you, you're really going to act like this?"

Script:

- "I appreciate everything you've done for me, but that doesn't mean I can't set boundaries or make decisions that feel right for me."
- "Gratitude doesn't mean ignoring my feelings or needs. Let's try to understand each other instead of focusing on guilt."

Why It Works:
This response acknowledges their efforts while reaffirming your right to prioritize your own needs.

4. Friendships and Social Circles

Gaslighting in friendships often involves subtle invalidation, competitiveness, or exclusion. These scripts help you address these behaviors diplomatically.

Scenario 1: Invalidating Your Achievements

Situation: A friend dismisses your accomplishment, saying, "That's not really a big deal. Anyone could do that."

Script:

- "It may not seem like a big deal to you, but it's important to me, and I'd appreciate your support."
- "It took a lot of effort for me to achieve this, and I'm proud of it. Let's celebrate together!"

Why It Works:
This response asserts your pride in your accomplishments and invites positivity, challenging their dismissiveness.

Scenario 2: Subtle Exclusion

Situation: A friend excludes you from plans and says, "We didn't think you'd be interested."

Script:

- "I understand you thought I might not be interested, but I'd like to be included in the future. I'll let you know if it's not my thing."
- "It feels hurtful to be left out. Let's work on communicating more openly about plans moving forward."

Why It Works:
This response expresses your feelings without assigning blame, encouraging more inclusive behavior.

5. General Strategies for Any Scenario
Stay Grounded in Facts

- "Let's stick to the facts so we can address the issue clearly."
- "I'm open to hearing your perspective, but I also need mine to be respected."

Deflect Personal Attacks

- "Let's focus on the issue, not personal criticism. I want to find a solution."
- "I don't think it's productive to attack each other. Let's talk about what's really bothering us."

Maintain Emotional Boundaries

- "I'm not comfortable continuing this conversation if my feelings are being dismissed."
- "I need some time to process this. Let's revisit it when we're both calmer."

6. When to Walk Away

Sometimes, the best response is no response. Walking away signals that you won't tolerate manipulative behavior.

- **How to Exit Calmly:**
    - "This conversation isn't productive right now. I'm stepping away and will return when we can talk respectfully."

- "I need to prioritize my well-being. Let's pause and revisit this later."

Boundary Setting 101: Step-by-Step Exercises for Establishing and Maintaining Limits

Boundaries are essential for protecting your mental health, maintaining autonomy, and fostering healthy relationships. They define what behaviors you will and won't accept and signal to others how you expect to be treated. This exercise-based guide walks you through the process of identifying, establishing, and maintaining boundaries step by step.

Step 1: Identify Your Boundaries

Understanding your limits is the foundation of boundary setting. Reflect on your values, needs, and past experiences to identify where boundaries are needed.

Exercise: "Boundary Map"

- **Materials Needed:** Pen and paper or a digital note-taking app.
- **Instructions:**
    1. Draw a circle and label it "My Safe Space."
    2. Outside the circle, write down behaviors, situations, or interactions that make you feel uncomfortable, disrespected, or drained. Examples:
        - Interrupting your personal time.
        - Dismissing your opinions.
        - Using guilt to influence your decisions.

3. Inside the circle, write down what makes you feel respected and valued. Examples:
   - Being listened to without interruption.
   - Having personal time honored.
   - Receiving constructive feedback.

Outcome: This exercise helps you visualize what you want to protect and what you need to limit in your interactions.

Step 2: Define Clear Boundaries

Once you've identified your needs, it's time to articulate specific boundaries for different areas of your life.

Exercise: "Boundary Script"

- **Materials Needed:** Pen and paper or a journal.
- **Instructions:**
   1. Write down one scenario where you feel a boundary is necessary.
      - Example: "A friend constantly asks me to do favors, even when I'm busy."
   2. Create a boundary statement using the formula: **"When [behavior happens], I feel [emotion], so I need [boundary]."**
      - Example: "When you ask for last-minute favors, I feel overwhelmed, so I need advance notice to consider helping."
   3. Repeat this process for other areas of your life, such as work, family, or romantic relationships.

Outcome: You'll have clear, actionable boundary statements that can be used in real-life situations.

Step 3: Communicate Your Boundaries

Communicating boundaries effectively requires assertiveness and clarity. Practice expressing your needs without apologizing or justifying them excessively.

Exercise: "Role-Playing Scenarios"

- **Materials Needed:** A trusted friend or a mirror.
- **Instructions:**
    1. Choose a boundary from your "Boundary Script" exercise.
    2. Role-play the scenario with a friend acting as the other person, or practice in front of a mirror.
        - Example: "I appreciate your input, but I need to make this decision on my own."
    3. Practice maintaining a calm, assertive tone. Avoid phrases like "I'm sorry, but…" or "I hate to say this…"
    4. Have your friend provide feedback or adjust your delivery based on how it feels to you.

Outcome: This exercise builds confidence in expressing boundaries and prepares you for real-life conversations.

Step 4: Anticipate Pushback

Some people may resist your boundaries, especially if they've benefited from you not having them in the past. Preparing for their reactions can help you stay firm.

Exercise: "Pushback Planner"

- **Materials Needed:** Pen and paper or a journal.
- **Instructions:**
    1. List potential reactions to your boundary, such as:
        - Guilt trips: "I can't believe you won't help me."
        - Anger: "You're being unreasonable."
        - Denial: "That's not what I meant to do."
    2. For each reaction, write a calm, assertive response. Examples:
        - Guilt trip: "I understand you're upset, but my decision stands."
        - Anger: "I won't engage in this conversation if it becomes disrespectful."
        - Denial: "That may not have been your intention, but this is how I feel."
    3. Practice delivering these responses to reinforce your confidence.

Outcome: You'll feel prepared to handle resistance without compromising your boundaries.

Step 5: Enforce Consequences

Enforcing boundaries requires follow-through. Clearly defined consequences reinforce the importance of your limits.

Exercise: "Consequences Checklist"

- **Materials Needed:** Pen and paper or a digital document.
- **Instructions:**
    1. Choose a boundary you want to enforce. Example: "No work calls after 7 PM."
    2. Define a specific consequence for when the boundary is violated. Example: "If I receive a work call after 7 PM, I will let it go to voicemail and address it the next morning."
    3. Write down the consequence next to the boundary for clarity.
    4. Practice enforcing these consequences consistently, reminding yourself that this is about self-respect, not punishment.

Outcome: You'll have a clear action plan for maintaining your boundaries and protecting your well-being.

Step 6: Reflect and Adjust

Boundary setting is a dynamic process. Over time, you may need to reevaluate and adjust your limits as your needs or relationships evolve.

Exercise: "Boundary Reflection Journal"

- **Materials Needed:** Journal or digital app.
- **Instructions:**
    1. At the end of each week, reflect on interactions where you set or enforced boundaries. Write answers to the following questions:
        - What worked well?
        - Where did I struggle?
        - How did setting this boundary make me feel?
    2. Identify areas for improvement or adjustments to your boundaries.
        - Example: "I realized I need to set clearer consequences for late-night texts."
    3. Celebrate your progress, even if it's small. Growth takes time!

Outcome: Regular reflection helps you refine your boundaries and reinforces your commitment to self-care.

Step 7: Strengthen Your Inner Confidence

Boundaries are easier to maintain when you trust yourself and your decisions. Building inner confidence ensures that you stay consistent.

Exercise: "Affirmation Practice"

- **Materials Needed:** Sticky notes or a journal.
- **Instructions:**

1. Write down affirmations that reinforce your right to set boundaries. Examples:
   - "I have the right to protect my time and energy."
   - "Saying no is an act of self-care, not selfishness."
   - "My boundaries are valid and deserve to be respected."
2. Place these affirmations where you'll see them daily or repeat them to yourself in moments of doubt.

Outcome: Affirmations strengthen your self-belief, making it easier to stand firm in your boundaries.

Maintaining Boundaries Long-Term

1. **Consistency is Key:** Stick to your boundaries, even when it feels uncomfortable. Over time, others will learn to respect them.
2. **Self-Compassion:** If you slip up, don't be hard on yourself. Boundary setting is a skill that takes practice.
3. **Support System:** Surround yourself with people who respect and encourage your limits.
4. **Celebrate Wins:** Acknowledge and celebrate each time you successfully set or enforce a boundary.

Visual Aids: Illustrating "Healthy vs. Toxic" Communication Patterns

Visual aids can be incredibly effective in highlighting the differences between healthy and toxic communication patterns.

Below are descriptions of diagrams that illustrate these contrasts, helping readers understand and recognize the dynamics of their interactions. You can visualize these concepts through flowcharts, side-by-side comparisons, and relational diagrams.

1. The Communication Flowchart
Purpose:

To show how messages are sent, received, and interpreted in healthy versus toxic communication.

Healthy Communication Flowchart

1. **Message Sent:** Speaker expresses their thoughts clearly and respectfully.
2. **Message Received:** Listener actively listens without interrupting.
3. **Feedback Given:** Listener reflects on what they heard, asking clarifying questions if needed.
4. **Resolution:** Both parties collaborate to address the issue or reach mutual understanding.

Flow Example:
Speaker → "I felt hurt when you canceled our plans last minute. Can we talk about it?"
Listener → "I'm sorry you felt that way. Can you tell me more about how it affected you?"

Toxic Communication Flowchart

1. **Message Sent:** Speaker communicates with blame or hostility.
2. **Message Received:** Listener reacts defensively or dismissively.
3. **Feedback Given:** Feedback is distorted or ignored, escalating the conflict.
4. **No Resolution:** Communication breaks down, leaving unresolved tension.

Flow Example:
Speaker → "You're so inconsiderate for canceling plans again. You never think about me!"
Listener → "You're overreacting. It wasn't a big deal."

Diagram Layout:
A linear flowchart with color-coded arrows (green for healthy and red for toxic) to visually separate the two pathways.

2. Side-by-Side Comparison: Healthy vs. Toxic Communication

Purpose:

To highlight the key differences in tone, intent, and outcomes between healthy and toxic communication.

Aspect	Healthy Communication	Toxic Communication
Tone	Calm, respectful, and empathetic.	Hostile, dismissive, or condescending.

Aspect	Healthy Communication	Toxic Communication
Intent	Seeks mutual understanding and resolution.	Aims to control, blame, or avoid responsibility.
Listening Style	Active listening with genuine interest in the other person's perspective.	Interrupts, dismisses, or ignores the other person's feelings.
Conflict Approach	Collaborative and solution-focused.	Escalates conflict or avoids addressing the issue.
Outcome	Strengthens trust and respect.	Erodes trust and creates resentment.

Diagram Layout:
A table or infographic with contrasting colors (e.g., green for healthy and red for toxic) and icons to visually emphasize the key points.

3. The "Feedback Loop" Diagram
Purpose:

To depict how communication patterns reinforce themselves in both healthy and toxic relationships.

Healthy Feedback Loop

1. **Expression:** Both individuals feel safe to express their thoughts and emotions.
2. **Validation:** Each person acknowledges the other's perspective without judgment.
3. **Adjustment:** Both adjust their behavior based on the feedback, fostering mutual growth.
4. **Positive Outcome:** The relationship becomes stronger and more trusting.

Flow Example:
Person A: "I feel overwhelmed when I'm left to handle everything alone."
Person B: "I hear you. I'll take on more responsibility so it's not all on you."

Toxic Feedback Loop

1. **Expression Suppressed:** One person dominates the conversation, or emotions are dismissed.
2. **Invalidation:** Feelings are belittled or ignored, creating frustration.
3. **Escalation:** Tensions rise as unresolved issues pile up.
4. **Negative Outcome:** Resentment and emotional distance grow over time.

Flow Example:
Person A: "I feel overwhelmed when I'm left to handle everything alone."
Person B: "You're always complaining. Maybe you should just deal with it."

Diagram Layout:
A circular diagram with arrows showing the continuous loop of feedback, with healthy loops shown in green and toxic loops in red.

4. "The Ladder of Communication" Diagram
Purpose:

To visually rank behaviors from constructive to destructive, emphasizing the difference between healthy and toxic communication.

Healthy Ladder: Steps to Connection

1. **Empathy:** "I see where you're coming from."
2. **Clarity:** "Here's how I feel and why."
3. **Validation:** "Your feelings are valid."
4. **Collaboration:** "Let's find a solution together."

Toxic Ladder: Steps to Disconnection

1. **Dismissiveness:** "You're overreacting."
2. **Defensiveness:** "It's not my fault."
3. **Criticism:** "You always mess things up."
4. **Contempt:** "I don't care what you think."

Diagram Layout:
Two ladders side by side, with healthy communication climbing upward (green) and toxic communication descending downward (red).

5. The "Emotional Exchange" Diagram
Purpose:

To illustrate how emotional energy is exchanged in healthy and toxic communication.

Healthy Emotional Exchange

- **Input:** Respect, empathy, and honesty.
- **Process:** Open dialogue with active listening.
- **Output:** Resolution, understanding, and emotional fulfillment.

Toxic Emotional Exchange

- **Input:** Blame, defensiveness, and dishonesty.
- **Process:** Miscommunication and invalidation.
- **Output:** Emotional exhaustion, frustration, and resentment.

Diagram Layout:
A scale with weights representing the balance in healthy communication and the imbalance in toxic communication. Use arrows to show how energy flows between individuals.

Chapter 6: Escaping Gaslighting Relationships

Leaving a gaslighting relationship is a challenging but liberating journey. Gaslighting thrives on control, manipulation, and eroding your sense of reality, making it difficult to break free. This chapter provides a comprehensive roadmap for recognizing when it's time to leave, preparing to do so safely, and rebuilding your life after escaping a toxic situation.

1. Recognizing the Need to Leave

The first step in escaping a gaslighting relationship is acknowledging its impact on your mental health, self-esteem, and overall well-being.

Signs It's Time to Leave:

- **Erosion of Self-Worth:** You feel constantly criticized, doubted, or dismissed.
- **Isolation:** The gaslighter has distanced you from friends, family, or support systems.
- **Constant Confusion:** You doubt your memory, decisions, or reality more often than not.
- **Emotional Exhaustion:** Interactions leave you drained, anxious, or fearful.
- **Lack of Growth:** The relationship stifles your personal development and happiness.

Reflection Exercise:

- Write down moments where you felt invalidated, controlled, or emotionally hurt by the gaslighter.
- Ask yourself, "Am I thriving or merely surviving in this relationship?"

Outcome: Recognizing these patterns will help solidify your decision to leave.

2. Planning Your Exit: Safety First

Leaving a gaslighting relationship can provoke strong reactions from the manipulator, especially if they fear losing control. A well-thought-out exit plan ensures your safety and stability.

Step 1: Build a Support System

- **Who to Trust:** Reach out to friends, family, or support groups who validate your experiences and respect your decisions.
- **What to Share:** Keep your plans private from the gaslighter to avoid interference.
- **Professional Support:** Consider working with a therapist who specializes in emotional abuse.

Step 2: Document Evidence

- Keep a record of manipulative behaviors, such as text messages, emails, or notes about interactions. This may be useful if you need to explain your situation to others or pursue legal action.

Step 3: Secure Financial and Practical Independence

- **Finances:** Open a separate bank account, save money discreetly, and gather financial documents (e.g., pay stubs, bank statements).
- **Essentials:** Pack a bag with important items like identification, legal documents, keys, and a few personal belongings in case you need to leave quickly.
- **Housing:** Research safe housing options, such as staying with a trusted friend or finding a shelter if necessary.

Step 4: Know Your Legal Rights

- Research local laws regarding restraining orders, custody arrangements (if applicable), and shared property.
- Consult a lawyer or advocate for advice tailored to your situation.

3. Setting Boundaries for Your Departure

Gaslighters may escalate manipulative tactics to regain control when they sense you're leaving. Clear boundaries help you navigate this transition with confidence.

Key Boundaries to Establish:

- **Limit Communication:** Use neutral, concise responses or go "no contact" if possible.
    - **Example:** "I've made my decision, and I need space to move forward."

- **Avoid Justification:** You don't owe the gaslighter an explanation for leaving.
    - **Example:** "This relationship isn't healthy for me, and I need to focus on myself."
- **Enforce Consequences:** If boundaries are violated, take action, such as blocking their number or seeking legal protection.

4. Rebuilding Your Life Post-Gaslighting

Leaving the relationship is only the beginning. Healing and rebuilding your confidence are essential steps toward reclaiming your autonomy and happiness.

Step 1: Prioritize Self-Care

- **Physical Health:** Exercise, eat well, and maintain a consistent sleep schedule to restore your energy.
- **Emotional Health:** Practice mindfulness, journaling, or meditation to process your emotions.
- **Self-Compassion:** Remind yourself that leaving was an act of strength and self-respect.

Step 2: Reconnect with Yourself

- **Revisit Passions:** Rediscover hobbies, interests, or activities that bring you joy.
- **Set Goals:** Focus on personal growth by setting achievable goals for your career, relationships, or self-improvement.

- **Affirm Your Identity:** Challenge negative beliefs instilled by the gaslighter by affirming your worth and capabilities.

Step 3: Build Healthy Relationships

- Surround yourself with people who respect your boundaries, validate your experiences, and uplift you.
- Learn to recognize the signs of healthy communication and mutual respect in future relationships.

Step 4: Seek Professional Support

- A therapist can help you unpack the trauma of gaslighting, rebuild self-trust, and develop tools for navigating future relationships.
- Join support groups for survivors of emotional abuse to connect with others who understand your journey.

5. Staying Free: Avoiding the Pull of the Gaslighter

Gaslighters may attempt to re-enter your life through charm, guilt, or false promises of change. Staying vigilant ensures you don't fall back into their cycle of manipulation.

Common Tactics Gaslighters Use Post-Breakup:

- **Love-Bombing:** Overwhelming you with affection or apologies to win you back.
- **Victimhood:** Claiming they're suffering without you or blaming you for their pain.

- **Smear Campaigns:** Spreading false narratives to damage your reputation or isolate you further.

How to Resist:

- **Stick to Boundaries:** Maintain "no contact" or minimal, neutral communication if necessary (e.g., for co-parenting).
- **Remember Your Why:** Reflect on the reasons you left and the progress you've made.
- **Lean on Support:** Seek encouragement from your trusted support system or therapist.

6. Thriving Beyond the Relationship

Escaping a gaslighting relationship is a transformative process that opens the door to a healthier, more fulfilling life. Use this time to rediscover your strength and purpose.

Tips for Thriving:

- **Celebrate Milestones:** Acknowledge every step forward, no matter how small.
- **Redefine Success:** Focus on your own happiness and personal growth instead of external validation.
- **Pay It Forward:** Share your story to inspire and support others who may be facing similar challenges.

Step-by-Step Guidance on Planning an Exit Strategy from a Gaslighting Relationship

Leaving a gaslighting relationship is a significant and empowering decision. However, it requires careful planning to ensure your safety, emotional well-being, and long-term stability. This step-by-step guide provides a detailed roadmap to create a practical and effective exit strategy, whether you're leaving a romantic relationship, workplace, or family dynamic.

Step 1: Acknowledge the Problem
Recognize Gaslighting Patterns

- Reflect on your relationship and identify gaslighting behaviors:
    - Are your feelings consistently dismissed or invalidated?
    - Do you feel confused or doubt your perceptions frequently?
    - Is there a pattern of control, manipulation, or isolation?

Affirm Your Decision to Leave

- Leaving a gaslighting relationship is not selfish or wrong—it's an act of self-care.
- Use affirmations like:
    - "I deserve to be treated with respect."
    - "My reality and feelings are valid."

Why This Step Matters:
Acknowledging the problem helps you overcome self-doubt and commit to taking action.

Step 2: Build a Support Network
Identify Trusted Allies

- Reach out to friends, family members, or colleagues who validate your experiences and offer emotional support.
- Consider joining support groups for individuals facing emotional abuse or manipulation.

Engage Professional Help

- Work with a therapist or counselor to navigate the emotional complexities of leaving.
- Consult a lawyer or advocate if legal assistance is required (e.g., restraining orders, custody arrangements).

Keep Your Plans Confidential

- Avoid sharing your intentions with the gaslighter or individuals who might relay information to them.

Why This Step Matters:
A strong support network provides emotional strength and practical guidance during your transition.

Step 3: Document Evidence
Record Manipulative Behavior

- Keep a journal detailing instances of gaslighting, including dates, events, and how it made you feel.
- Save text messages, emails, or voicemails that demonstrate manipulation, threats, or coercion.

Why This Is Useful

- Documentation may be critical for legal actions, custody disputes, or explaining your decision to others.

Step 4: Secure Financial Independence
Assess Your Financial Situation

- Review your current income, savings, and expenses.
- Create a budget for post-relationship living, including housing, utilities, and necessities.

Take Practical Steps

- Open a separate bank account in your name and begin saving discreetly.
- Gather financial documents, such as:
    - Pay stubs
    - Tax returns
    - Bank statements
    - Credit reports

Why This Step Matters:
Financial independence reduces your reliance on the gaslighter and ensures stability after leaving.

Step 5: Prepare Your Essentials
Pack an Emergency Bag

- Include items you might need if you have to leave quickly, such as:
    - Identification (passport, driver's license)
    - Legal documents (birth certificate, marriage license, custody papers)
    - Medication and medical records
    - A few days' worth of clothes and toiletries
    - Cash or bank cards

Gather Important Information

- Write down emergency contact numbers, account details, and passwords.
- Back up critical documents digitally or store them with a trusted friend.

Why This Step Matters:
Having essentials ready ensures you can leave swiftly and reduces the risk of leaving behind important items.

Step 6: Plan for Safe Housing
Evaluate Your Options

- Stay with a trusted friend or family member who supports your decision.

- Research local shelters or organizations that provide housing for individuals leaving abusive relationships.

Secure Your New Location

- Ensure your new residence is unknown to the gaslighter to minimize the risk of harassment or confrontation.
- Inform your support network of your location and any safety concerns.

Why This Step Matters:
A secure and stable living arrangement provides a foundation for rebuilding your life.

Step 7: Create a Communication Plan
Decide on Post-Exit Communication

- **No Contact:** In many cases, cutting off communication is the healthiest option.
- **Low Contact:** If necessary (e.g., for co-parenting or legal matters), keep communication minimal, neutral, and focused on logistics.

Set Boundaries

- Use concise and assertive language:
    - "I've made my decision, and I won't discuss it further."
    - "Please respect my boundaries by contacting me only for essential matters."

Consider Technology

- Block the gaslighter's number and social media profiles if appropriate.
- Use a new phone number or email address for private communication.

Why This Step Matters:
Controlling communication reduces the gaslighter's ability to manipulate or guilt you into returning.

Step 8: Anticipate Pushback

Gaslighters often escalate their behavior when they sense they're losing control. Preparing for these tactics helps you stay resolute.

Common Tactics to Expect:

- **Love-Bombing:** Showering you with affection or promises to change.
- **Guilt Trips:** Blaming you for their behavior or claiming they can't live without you.
- **Threats:** Intimidating you with consequences if you leave.
- **Smear Campaigns:** Spreading false narratives about you to mutual acquaintances.

How to Respond:

- Stay firm in your decision. Repeat: "This decision is final and non-negotiable."

- Rely on your support network or seek professional advice if you feel unsafe.

Why This Step Matters:
Anticipating and preparing for manipulation tactics reduces their emotional impact.

Step 9: Execute Your Exit
Choose the Right Time

- Pick a moment when the gaslighter is less likely to intervene, such as when they're away from home or work.

Inform Trusted Allies

- Let your support network know when you plan to leave so they can assist or check on you.

Leave Swiftly and Quietly

- Avoid confrontation or drawn-out explanations. Focus on your safety and well-being.

Why This Step Matters:
Executing your exit efficiently minimizes conflict and risk.

Step 10: Focus on Healing
Seek Therapy

- Work with a therapist to address the trauma of gaslighting and rebuild self-esteem.

Reconnect with Yourself

- Rediscover hobbies, interests, and relationships that bring you joy and fulfillment.

Set Goals

- Create short- and long-term goals to rebuild your life, such as pursuing a new career, strengthening friendships, or fostering self-confidence.

Why This Step Matters:
Healing is an ongoing process that allows you to reclaim your sense of self and move forward with confidence.

Resource List for Legal and Emotional Support

When dealing with gaslighting or any form of manipulation, having access to the right resources can make a significant difference in navigating your situation. This comprehensive list includes organizations, hotlines, and tools for both legal and emotional support, empowering you to take informed steps toward recovery and independence.

1. Legal Support Resources

Legal challenges, such as restraining orders, custody disputes, or financial independence, may arise when escaping a gaslighting relationship. The following resources can help:

Domestic Violence and Abuse Legal Assistance

- **National Domestic Violence Hotline (U.S.)**
  - Website: www.thehotline.org
  - Phone: 1-800-799-SAFE (7233)
  - Services: Offers free legal guidance, connects you with local attorneys, and provides safety planning resources.
- **Women's Law**
  - Website: www.womenslaw.org
  - Services: Provides legal information on restraining orders, custody, and divorce. Includes a secure email hotline for legal questions.
- **Legal Aid Societies**
  - Search for local legal aid organizations that provide free or low-cost legal assistance to those experiencing abuse.

Employment and Workplace Gaslighting

- **Equal Employment Opportunity Commission (EEOC)**
  - Website: www.eeoc.gov
  - Services: Protects workers from discrimination and retaliation in the workplace. File complaints about toxic work environments.
- **Workplace Fairness**
  - Website: www.workplacefairness.org
  - Services: Offers resources on employee rights, workplace harassment, and wrongful termination.

Restraining Orders and Custody

- **FindLaw**
    - Website: www.findlaw.com
    - Services: Provides easy-to-understand legal information on restraining orders, custody, and family law matters.
- **National Coalition Against Domestic Violence (NCADV)**
    - Website: www.ncadv.org
    - Services: Connects you with advocates who can help file protective orders and navigate custody disputes.

2. Emotional Support Resources

Dealing with the emotional aftermath of gaslighting requires compassionate and professional support. These resources can help you cope and heal.

Hotlines for Immediate Emotional Support

- **National Suicide Prevention Lifeline (U.S.)**
    - Website: www.988lifeline.org
    - Phone: Dial 988
    - Services: 24/7 confidential support for individuals in emotional distress.
- **Crisis Text Line (Global)**
    - Website: www.crisistextline.org
    - Text: HOME to 741741
    - Services: Free text-based support available 24/7.
- **SAMHSA's National Helpline**

- Website: www.samhsa.gov
- Phone: 1-800-662-HELP (4357)
- Services: Provides referrals to mental health and substance abuse treatment centers.

Therapy and Counseling Services

- **Psychology Today's Therapist Directory**
    - Website: www.psychologytoday.com
    - Services: Search for therapists by location, specialty, and insurance coverage.
- **BetterHelp**
    - Website: www.betterhelp.com
    - Services: Online therapy platform offering access to licensed counselors.
- **Talkspace**
    - Website: www.talkspace.com
    - Services: Text, video, or voice therapy with licensed professionals, tailored to your schedule.

Support Groups

- **Domestic Shelters**
    - Website: www.domesticshelters.org
    - Services: Find local and online support groups for survivors of abuse.
- **RAINN (Rape, Abuse & Incest National Network)**
    - Website: www.rainn.org
    - Phone: 1-800-656-HOPE (4673)
    - Services: Offers support groups and one-on-one chats for survivors of abuse and trauma.
- **Survivors of Incest Anonymous (SIA)**
    - Website: www.siawso.org

- Services: 12-step recovery groups for survivors of childhood abuse and trauma.

3. Online Resources for Education and Healing

Gaining knowledge about gaslighting and emotional abuse can empower you to take action and heal.

Educational Websites

- **The Gaslight Effect by Dr. Robin Stern**
  - Website: www.robinstern.com
  - Services: Articles and tools on recognizing and addressing gaslighting.
- **PsychCentral**
  - Website: www.psychcentral.com
  - Services: Mental health resources and articles on overcoming manipulation.
- **Love Is Respect**
  - Website: www.loveisrespect.org
  - Services: Focuses on healthy relationships and identifying toxic behaviors.

Books on Gaslighting and Emotional Recovery

- *The Gaslight Effect: How to Spot and Survive the Hidden Manipulation Others Use to Control Your Life* by Dr. Robin Stern.
- *Why Does He Do That? Inside the Minds of Angry and Controlling Men* by Lundy Bancroft.

- *Healing from Hidden Abuse: A Journey Through the Stages of Recovery from Psychological Abuse* by Shannon Thomas.

4. Resources for Building Safety Plans

If you're preparing to leave a gaslighting relationship, creating a safety plan is critical.

- **Safety Planning Tools**
    - **My Plan App** (Available on Android and iOS)
        - Helps you assess the safety of your relationship and create a personalized action plan.
    - **Love is Respect Safety Planning Guide**
        - Website: www.loveisrespect.org/safety-plan
        - Offers a detailed guide for leaving abusive relationships safely.
- **Shelters and Housing Assistance**
    - **National Network to End Domestic Violence (NNEDV)**
        - Website: www.nnedv.org
        - Services: Provides resources for finding safe shelters and housing options.
    - **Safe Horizon**
        - Website: www.safehorizon.org
        - Services: Assists with emergency housing and relocation support.

5. Resources for Children and Families

If children are involved, their safety and well-being should also be prioritized.

- **Childhelp National Child Abuse Hotline**
  - Website: www.childhelp.org
  - Phone: 1-800-4-A-CHILD (422-4453)
  - Services: Crisis intervention and resources for protecting children from abuse.
- **Parenting Support**
  - **One Tough Job**
    - Website: www.onetoughjob.org
    - Services: Resources for managing parenting challenges in toxic environments.

6. International Resources

If you're outside the U.S., these international resources can provide guidance and support:

- **Domestic Violence Hotlines by Country**
  - Website: www.hotpeachpages.net
  - Services: A directory of domestic violence resources worldwide.
- **Global Crisis Helplines**
  - Website: www.iasp.info/resources/Crisis_Centres
  - Services: Connects individuals to crisis centers and hotlines globally.

Strategies for Handling the Aftermath of Gaslighting: Smear Campaigns and Emotional Manipulation Attempts

Escaping a gaslighting relationship is a monumental step toward reclaiming your autonomy and mental health, but the aftermath can be equally challenging. Gaslighters often attempt to regain control through tactics like smear campaigns and emotional manipulation. Knowing how to navigate these challenges will help you maintain your boundaries, rebuild your confidence, and protect your reputation.

1. Understanding the Gaslighter's Tactics

Gaslighters rarely accept losing control without a fight. Their tactics often escalate after you leave, as they seek to regain dominance or discredit you.

Common Tactics in the Aftermath:

- **Smear Campaigns:** Spreading lies or half-truths about you to mutual acquaintances, colleagues, or family to tarnish your reputation.
- **Love-Bombing:** Showering you with affection, apologies, or promises to change to lure you back.
- **Playing the Victim:** Claiming they were wronged or mistreated to gain sympathy from others.
- **Emotional Blackmail:** Using guilt, fear, or obligation to manipulate you into re-engaging.
- **Triangulation:** Involving third parties to pressure or manipulate you.

Why They Do It:
Gaslighters fear losing control and often escalate their behavior to protect their ego and narrative.

2. Strategies for Handling Smear Campaigns

Step 1: Stay Calm and Grounded

- **Why:** Reacting emotionally can play into the gaslighter's narrative and reinforce their claims.
- **How:** Practice deep breathing, mindfulness, or journaling to process your emotions privately.

Step 2: Document the Smear Campaign

- Keep a record of false claims, slanderous statements, or any damaging rumors they spread.
- Save screenshots of social media posts, emails, or text messages as evidence if legal action becomes necessary.

Step 3: Focus on Your Integrity

- Avoid getting drawn into arguments or retaliating. Maintain your composure and focus on living authentically.
- **Example Response:** "I understand there are rumors, but I'm focusing on my own growth and well-being. The truth will speak for itself."

Step 4: Control Your Narrative

- Address the smear campaign selectively:

- Speak directly to those who are affected by the rumors or who matter most to you.
- Share only necessary information to clarify misunderstandings without overexplaining.
- **Example Response:** "I've heard about the rumors, and while I'm not here to engage in gossip, I want to assure you that I'm moving forward in a positive direction."

Step 5: Seek Legal Advice if Necessary

- If the smear campaign includes defamation, harassment, or endangers your safety, consult a lawyer to explore options like cease-and-desist letters or legal action.

3. Strategies for Handling Emotional Manipulation Attempts
Step 1: Enforce No-Contact or Low-Contact Rules

- **No-Contact:** Block their phone number, email, and social media accounts to eliminate their influence entirely.
- **Low-Contact:** If contact is unavoidable (e.g., co-parenting), use neutral, concise communication focused solely on necessary topics.
    - **Example Script:** "Please keep our communication limited to [specific topic]. I won't respond to anything unrelated."

Step 2: Recognize Manipulation Tactics

- **Love-Bombing:** They might say, "I've changed. Let's try again."

- **Response:** "I appreciate your apology, but my decision to move forward remains unchanged."
- **Playing the Victim:** They might claim, "You've ruined my life by leaving me."
    - **Response:** "I'm sorry you feel that way, but I'm prioritizing my own well-being."

Step 3: Use the "Gray Rock" Method

- **What It Is:** A technique where you remain emotionally unresponsive to manipulative tactics, making interactions uninteresting to the gaslighter.
- **How to Apply:**
    - Keep your responses short and factual.
    - Avoid reacting to provocations or attempts to draw you into emotional exchanges.
    - **Example Script:** "I have no comment on that."

Step 4: Prepare for Guilt-Tripping

- **What They Say:** "You're abandoning me when I need you most."
- **How to Respond:** "I'm sorry you feel that way, but I need to focus on my own growth."

4. Protecting Your Emotional Health
Step 1: Rebuild Your Self-Esteem

- Engage in activities that boost your confidence and sense of self-worth, such as:
    - Setting and achieving personal goals.

- Pursuing hobbies or interests you put aside during the relationship.
- Practicing affirmations like, "I deserve healthy, respectful relationships."

Step 2: Establish a Support Network

- Surround yourself with people who validate your experiences and encourage your growth.
- Join support groups for survivors of gaslighting or emotional abuse to connect with others who understand your journey.

Step 3: Seek Professional Help

- A therapist can help you unpack the trauma of gaslighting and develop coping strategies for the aftermath.
- Cognitive-behavioral therapy (CBT) or trauma-focused therapy can help you reframe negative thought patterns.

Step 4: Practice Self-Care

- Prioritize activities that nourish your mental and physical well-being, such as:
  - Regular exercise.
  - Mindfulness practices like meditation or journaling.
  - Maintaining a healthy sleep schedule and diet.

5. Navigating Relationships with Mutual Connections

Gaslighters often use mutual friends or acquaintances to spread their narrative or apply indirect pressure.

Step 1: Communicate Selectively

- Share your side of the story with those you trust but avoid oversharing or engaging in gossip.

Step 2: Set Boundaries with Mutual Connections

- Politely decline conversations about the gaslighter.
    - **Example Script:** "I'd rather not discuss that topic. Let's focus on something else."

Step 3: Distance Yourself if Necessary

- If mutual connections side with the gaslighter or perpetuate their narrative, consider limiting your interactions with them.

6. Focus on Long-Term Healing
Step 1: Celebrate Your Progress

- Acknowledge milestones, no matter how small, such as:
    - A week of no contact.
    - Reconnecting with a hobby or passion.
    - Feeling more confident in your decisions.

Step 2: Set New Goals

- Shift your focus toward future-oriented goals, such as:
    - Advancing your career.
    - Strengthening relationships with supportive individuals.
    - Exploring new hobbies or interests.

Step 3: Rebuild Your Identity

- Rediscover your values, preferences, and aspirations that may have been overshadowed by the gaslighting relationship.

Chapter 7: Rebuilding Your Identity and Confidence

Gaslighting erodes self-esteem, distorts reality, and often leaves victims questioning their worth and identity. Rebuilding your confidence and rediscovering who you are is a powerful and transformative journey. This chapter provides actionable steps, exercises, and strategies to help you reconnect with yourself, regain self-trust, and rebuild your confidence after experiencing gaslighting.

1. Understanding the Impact of Gaslighting on Identity
How Gaslighting Affects Your Sense of Self

- **Self-Doubt:** Constant manipulation leads to questioning your decisions, memories, and feelings.
- **Loss of Confidence:** Repeated invalidation diminishes your belief in your abilities.
- **Fragmented Identity:** The gaslighter may have imposed their version of who you are, making it hard to recognize your true self.

Recognizing the Damage

- Write down how gaslighting has affected your thoughts, emotions, and behaviors.
  - **Example:** "I hesitate to make decisions because I fear they'll be criticized."
- Acknowledge that these effects are not your fault—they're the result of manipulation.

2. Rebuilding Self-Trust

Reestablishing trust in yourself is the foundation of rediscovering your identity.

Exercise: Reality Validation

1. **Document Your Experiences:**
   - Keep a journal of daily events and how you perceive them.
   - Reflect on your emotions and why you felt a certain way.
2. **Cross-Check with Evidence:**
   - Refer to tangible evidence (e.g., emails, photos) to affirm your reality.
3. **Celebrate Accuracy:**
   - Acknowledge moments when your perceptions aligned with reality to reinforce self-trust.

Outcome: Regularly affirming your reality strengthens your confidence in your judgment.

Exercise: "Trust Yourself Again" Decisions

1. Start with small decisions, such as choosing what to eat or wear.
2. Gradually progress to larger decisions, like setting goals or pursuing interests.
3. Each time you make a choice, affirm: "I trust my instincts and decisions."

Outcome: Making intentional choices rebuilds your autonomy and decision-making confidence.

3. Rediscovering Your Identity

Gaslighting often blurs the lines between who you are and who the gaslighter wanted you to be. Rediscovering your authentic self is a liberating process.

Step 1: Reconnect with Your Values

- Reflect on what matters most to you—your beliefs, passions, and priorities.
    - **Prompt:** "What do I value in relationships, work, and life?"
- Write down your core values and how you can align your actions with them.

Step 2: Revisit Old Interests

- Recall hobbies, activities, or passions you enjoyed before the gaslighting relationship.
- Set aside time each week to explore or re-engage with these interests.

Step 3: Define Who You Are

- Complete the statement: "I am someone who values _____ and enjoys _____."
- Revise this statement as you grow and rediscover more about yourself.

4. Rebuilding Confidence

Confidence grows when you take actions that affirm your abilities and worth.

Step 1: Set Achievable Goals

- Start with small, manageable goals that you can accomplish within a short timeframe.
    - **Example:** "I'll spend 30 minutes practicing a hobby this week."
- Gradually increase the complexity of your goals as your confidence builds.

Step 2: Acknowledge Your Strengths

- List skills, qualities, or achievements you're proud of—even small ones.
    - **Example:** "I'm great at organizing events" or "I helped a friend through a tough time."
- Revisit this list regularly to remind yourself of your capabilities.

Step 3: Challenge Negative Self-Talk

- Recognize critical thoughts and replace them with affirmations.
    - Instead of: "I'm not good enough," say, "I'm learning and growing every day."
- Write affirmations on sticky notes and place them where you'll see them often.

5. Reclaiming Independence

Gaslighting fosters dependency on the manipulator. Reclaiming your independence is crucial for rebuilding your confidence.

Step 1: Develop New Skills

- Take a course or learn something new to expand your abilities.
    - **Example:** Learn a new language, pick up a craft, or improve professional skills.
- Celebrate progress, no matter how small.

Step 2: Create Routines

- Establish daily or weekly routines that prioritize your needs and interests.
    - **Example:** A morning routine that includes meditation, exercise, and goal-setting.
- Routines provide stability and reinforce your sense of control.

Step 3: Manage Your Time and Space

- Organize your environment to reflect your preferences and identity.
    - **Example:** Decorate your living space in a way that makes you feel at peace.
- Schedule time for self-care, hobbies, and meaningful activities.

6. Strengthening Relationships

Healthy relationships are integral to rebuilding confidence and identity.

Step 1: Seek Supportive Connections

- Surround yourself with people who respect your boundaries and validate your experiences.
- Join support groups or communities aligned with your interests and values.

Step 2: Set Relationship Boundaries

- Define what behaviors you will and won't tolerate in future relationships.
    - **Example:** "I will only engage in conversations that are respectful and constructive."
- Practice asserting these boundaries with confidence.

Step 3: Foster Mutual Respect

- Prioritize relationships where communication, trust, and empathy are mutual.
- Let go of connections that drain your energy or perpetuate toxicity.

7. Embracing Growth and Healing

Recovery from gaslighting is an ongoing journey of growth and self-discovery.

Step 1: Reflect on Progress

- Keep a journal of your milestones and accomplishments.
  - **Example:** "Today, I stood up for myself in a conversation."
- Use these reflections as reminders of your resilience.

Step 2: Celebrate Yourself

- Reward yourself for reaching goals, no matter how small.
  - Treat yourself to something you enjoy, like a favorite meal or a relaxing activity.

Step 3: Accept Imperfection

- Embrace the idea that healing is not linear and that setbacks are part of the process.
- Be gentle with yourself, recognizing that growth takes time.

8. Looking Ahead

Rebuilding your identity and confidence after gaslighting is about creating a life that reflects your values, passions, and authentic self.

Step 1: Define Your Vision

- Write a vision statement for your future.
  - **Example:** "I see myself as confident, independent, and surrounded by supportive relationships."

Step 2: Take Ownership of Your Story

- Share your experiences with others when you're ready, using your journey to inspire or help others.
- Recognize that your story is one of resilience, strength, and transformation.

Tools for Reframing Negative Self-Talk and Boosting Self-Worth

Negative self-talk often lingers long after experiencing gaslighting or other forms of emotional manipulation, eroding self-worth and fostering doubt. Reframing these harmful thoughts and actively boosting self-esteem are crucial steps toward healing and empowerment. Below are effective tools and exercises designed to help you shift your mindset, nurture self-worth, and rebuild confidence.

1. Recognize and Label Negative Self-Talk

The first step in reframing negative thoughts is to identify them and understand their origins.

Tool: Negative Thought Journal

- **What It Is:** A tool to document and analyze your negative thoughts to uncover patterns and triggers.
- **How to Use:**
    1. Carry a journal or use a notes app on your phone.
    2. Each time you notice negative self-talk, write it down. Include:
        - The thought: *"I'm not good enough."*

- The trigger: *"I made a mistake at work."*
- The emotion: *"Embarrassment, fear of judgment."*
  3. Reflect weekly to identify recurring themes.
- **Outcome:** Increased awareness of how negative self-talk operates in your mind, making it easier to challenge.

2. Reframe Negative Thoughts with Evidence-Based Counterarguments

Replace distorted thoughts with balanced, evidence-based perspectives.

Tool: Thought Reframing Chart

- **What It Is:** A structured chart that helps you transform negative thoughts into positive or neutral ones.
- **How to Use:**
  1. Divide a page into three columns:
     - Negative Thought: *"I always fail at everything."*
     - Evidence Against This Thought: *"I successfully completed a major project last month."*
     - Reframed Thought: *"I may make mistakes sometimes, but I'm capable of succeeding."*
  2. Complete the chart for each recurring negative thought.
- **Outcome:** Encourages logical, compassionate thinking and reduces the emotional weight of negativity.

3. Practice Self-Compassion

Self-compassion involves treating yourself with the same kindness you'd offer a close friend.

Tool: Self-Compassion Statements

- **What It Is:** Affirmations designed to foster a gentler, more forgiving mindset.
- **How to Use:**
    1. When negative self-talk arises, respond with self-compassion:
        - *Negative Thought:* "I'm so stupid for making that mistake."
        - *Self-Compassionate Response:* "Everyone makes mistakes. This is part of learning and growing."
    2. Repeat these statements until they feel more natural.
- **Outcome:** Reduces self-criticism and encourages emotional resilience.

4. Replace Critical Inner Dialogue with Affirmations

Affirmations are powerful tools for shifting your mindset and reinforcing positive beliefs.

Tool: Personalized Affirmation Practice

- **What It Is:** Creating and repeating affirmations tailored to your specific needs and goals.
- **How to Use:**

1. Write down areas where you feel inadequate or doubt yourself.
   - **Example:** *"I feel like I'm not confident enough."*
2. Create affirmations that counter these thoughts:
   - *"I am learning to trust myself and grow in confidence every day."*
3. Repeat affirmations daily, ideally in front of a mirror or as part of a morning routine.
- **Outcome:** Gradually replaces negative beliefs with empowering ones, boosting self-worth.

5. Cultivate Gratitude

Focusing on what you appreciate about yourself and your life helps shift attention away from negativity.

Tool: Gratitude and Strength Journal

- **What It Is:** A journal to document things you're grateful for and personal strengths.
- **How to Use:**
  1. Each day, write down:
     - Three things you're grateful for.
     - One thing you did well or are proud of.
     - One personal quality you value in yourself.
  2. Reflect on your entries weekly to notice patterns and areas of growth.
- **Outcome:** Reinforces a positive self-image and promotes a mindset of abundance.

6. Reframe Comparisons

Comparing yourself to others often fuels feelings of inadequacy. Reframing comparisons helps shift the focus back to your unique strengths and journey.

Tool: The "Me vs. Me" Approach

- **What It Is:** A mindset shift from comparing yourself to others to comparing your present self to your past self.
- **How to Use:**
    1. Identify moments when you compare yourself to someone else.
        - **Example:** "They're so much more successful than I am."
    2. Reframe by reflecting on your own progress:
        - *"I've grown so much over the past year. I'm on my own unique path."*
    3. Celebrate milestones, no matter how small.
- **Outcome:** Reduces external validation dependency and highlights your personal growth.

7. Build Confidence Through Small Wins

Achieving small, realistic goals reinforces a sense of competence and self-worth.

Tool: Confidence Ladder

- **What It Is:** A step-by-step plan to tackle challenges and build confidence incrementally.
- **How to Use:**

1. Identify a goal that feels overwhelming (e.g., giving a presentation at work).
2. Break it into smaller, manageable steps (e.g., practicing with a friend, rehearsing in front of a mirror).
3. Celebrate each step you complete, regardless of the outcome.
- **Outcome:** Reinforces the belief that you're capable of growth and success.

8. Visualize Success

Visualization helps train your brain to focus on positive outcomes and reinforce confidence.

Tool: Guided Visualization Exercise

- **What It Is:** A mental practice of envisioning your best self succeeding.
- **How to Use:**
    1. Find a quiet space and close your eyes.
    2. Visualize yourself confidently handling a challenge, such as acing a job interview or asserting a boundary.
    3. Focus on the emotions of success—pride, confidence, and relief.
    4. Repeat this exercise daily to embed the positive image in your mind.
- **Outcome:** Prepares you mentally for challenges and strengthens your belief in your abilities.

9. Surround Yourself with Positivity

Your environment significantly impacts your mindset and self-worth.

Tool: Positive Influences Checklist

- **What It Is:** A tool to evaluate and curate your social, physical, and mental environment.
- **How to Use:**
    1. List people, activities, and media that uplift you.
        - **Example:** "Spending time with supportive friends, listening to motivational podcasts."
    2. List those that drain or discourage you.
        - **Example:** "Engaging in toxic conversations, doom-scrolling social media."
    3. Commit to increasing positive influences and minimizing negative ones.
- **Outcome:** Creates an environment that nurtures self-worth and positivity.

10. Practice Self-Validation

Relying on external validation can undermine your confidence. Learning to self-validate builds inner strength.

Tool: Self-Validation Statements

- **What It Is:** Affirming your worth and decisions without external input.

- **How to Use:**
    1. When faced with self-doubt, write a statement affirming your value:
        - *"I did my best today, and that's enough."*
    2. Reflect on situations where you acted with integrity or courage and acknowledge your effort.
- **Outcome:** Reinforces your ability to validate yourself, reducing reliance on others for approval.

Exercises: "Who Am I?" — Rediscovering Personal Values, Preferences, and Strengths

After experiencing gaslighting or other forms of emotional manipulation, it's common to feel disconnected from your sense of self. Rediscovering your values, preferences, and strengths is a transformative journey that rebuilds your identity and confidence. The following exercises are designed to help you explore who you truly are, reconnect with your authentic self, and embrace your unique qualities.

1. The Values Compass: Defining Your Core Principles
Purpose:

To identify the guiding principles that shape your decisions and give your life meaning.

Steps:

1. **List Potential Values:** Write down a list of values that resonate with you. Examples include:
    - Integrity
    - Creativity

- Family
- Freedom
- Growth
- Compassion
- Adventure
- Honesty

2. **Reflect on Past Experiences:**
   - Think of moments when you felt fulfilled or proud.
   - Ask yourself: "What value was I honoring in that moment?"
   - **Example:** "When I volunteered at the shelter, I was honoring compassion and community."

3. **Prioritize Your Top Values:**
   - Narrow your list down to 5-7 core values that feel most important.

4. **Align Your Actions:**
   - For each value, write down one way you can incorporate it into your daily life.
   - **Example:** For "creativity," dedicate time to writing, painting, or brainstorming new ideas.

Outcome:

A clear understanding of what matters most to you, providing a foundation for authentic decision-making.

2. The Preference Palette: Exploring What Brings You Joy

Purpose:

To rediscover the activities, environments, and experiences that make you happy.

Steps:

1. **Create a "Joy Journal":**
    - Over the course of a week, note activities, places, or interactions that made you feel energized, peaceful, or joyful.
    - Include small moments, like enjoying a cup of coffee or walking in nature.
2. **Reflect on Patterns:**
    - Review your journal entries and identify recurring themes.
    - **Example:** "I feel happiest when I'm spending time outdoors or listening to music."
3. **Revisit Childhood Favorites:**
    - List activities or hobbies you loved as a child but may have abandoned.
    - **Example:** Drawing, dancing, building models, or storytelling.
4. **Experiment with New Activities:**
    - Choose one activity each week to try or revisit. Note how it makes you feel.
    - **Example:** Attend a pottery class, visit a museum, or learn a new skill.

Outcome:

A deeper understanding of what excites and fulfills you, helping you prioritize these elements in your life.

3. The Strength Snapshot: Recognizing Your Unique Talents

Purpose:

To identify your personal strengths and skills, reinforcing confidence in your abilities.

Steps:

1. **Ask Reflective Questions:**
    - "What have others complimented me on?"
    - "When have I felt most successful?"
    - "What tasks or challenges do I handle well?"
2. **Review Past Accomplishments:**
    - Write down three to five achievements you're proud of.
    - For each, identify the strengths you used to achieve them.
    - **Example:** "I organized a charity event, which showed my skills in planning, leadership, and communication."
3. **Take a Strengths Assessment:**
    - Use free online tools like the VIA Character Strengths Survey or StrengthsFinder to gain additional insights.
4. **Create a Strength Statement:**
    - Combine your top strengths into a statement:

- *"I am resourceful, empathetic, and creative, and I use these strengths to solve problems and connect with others."*

Outcome:

A clear picture of your abilities, boosting self-confidence and guiding you in leveraging your strengths.

4. The "Me Map": Visualizing Your Identity
Purpose:

To create a visual representation of who you are, encompassing your values, preferences, and strengths.

Steps:

1. **Draw Your Map:**
   - In the center of a blank sheet, write your name and draw a circle around it.
2. **Add Branches:**
   - Around the circle, create branches for categories such as:
     - Values
     - Interests
     - Strengths
     - Goals
3. **Fill in Each Category:**
   - Under each branch, write down relevant items.
   - *Example:* Under "Values," write "compassion," "honesty," and "freedom." Under "Strengths," write "problem-solving" and "communication."

4. **Decorate Your Map:**
    - Use colors, images, or symbols that represent your personality.
    - Make it visually appealing so it inspires you.

Outcome:

A tangible reminder of your unique qualities and aspirations that you can revisit whenever you feel uncertain.

5. The Authentic Self Checklist
Purpose:

To assess whether your current lifestyle aligns with your rediscovered identity.

Steps:

1. **Write Down Key Aspects of Your Identity:**
    - Include your values, preferences, and strengths.
2. **Evaluate Your Current Life:**
    - For each aspect, ask:
        - "Am I honoring this value in my daily life?"
        - "Am I using this strength regularly?"
        - "Am I prioritizing activities that align with my preferences?"
3. **Create an Action Plan:**
    - Identify areas where you're out of alignment and set small, actionable goals to make changes.

- *Example:* If freedom is a core value, consider setting boundaries to protect your time or exploring flexible career options.

Outcome:

A roadmap for living in alignment with your true self.

6. The Vision Board: Envisioning Your Best Self
Purpose:

To create a visual representation of your goals, dreams, and identity.

Steps:

1. **Gather Supplies:**
   - Use a corkboard, poster board, or a digital platform like Pinterest.
2. **Find Inspiration:**
   - Collect images, quotes, and symbols that resonate with your values, preferences, and strengths.
   - *Example:* A mountain for adventure, a quote about self-love, or photos of meaningful achievements.
3. **Organize Your Vision:**
   - Arrange your items into categories, such as personal growth, relationships, career, and hobbies.
4. **Display Your Vision Board:**

- Place it somewhere you'll see it daily to reinforce your goals and aspirations.

Outcome:

A visual guide to motivate and inspire you as you rediscover and embrace your authentic self.

7. The Identity Timeline
Purpose:

To trace your journey and identify defining moments that have shaped your identity.

Steps:

1. **Create a Timeline:**
   - Draw a horizontal line across a page, marking key stages of your life (childhood, adolescence, adulthood).
2. **Identify Defining Moments:**
   - Note experiences that influenced your values, preferences, or strengths.
   - *Example:* "Volunteering in high school taught me the value of service."
3. **Highlight Lessons Learned:**
   - For each moment, write what you learned about yourself.
   - *Example:* "When I overcame a tough breakup, I discovered my resilience."
4. **Reflect on Your Growth:**

- Review your timeline to appreciate how far you've come.

Outcome:

A clearer understanding of your journey and the qualities that make you unique.

Inspirational Stories of Transformation and Recovery

Transformation and recovery after experiencing gaslighting or emotional manipulation can feel like an uphill battle. However, these inspiring stories of resilience, healing, and empowerment demonstrate that it is possible to reclaim your identity, rebuild your confidence, and create a fulfilling life. While fictionalized to protect privacy, these narratives are rooted in real experiences of courage and growth.

1. Emily's Story: From Self-Doubt to Self-Empowerment
The Challenge

Emily, a 35-year-old graphic designer, spent years in a relationship with a partner who constantly invalidated her feelings and undermined her achievements. Phrases like "You're overreacting" or "You'd be nothing without me" eroded her confidence, leaving her questioning her worth and abilities.

The Turning Point

One evening, after her partner dismissed her excitement over landing a major client, Emily confided in a coworker. Her coworker's validation of her talent sparked a realization: she had been allowing someone else's narrative to define her value.

The Recovery

Emily began her journey to recovery by:

- **Seeking Therapy:** A therapist helped her recognize patterns of gaslighting and develop tools to rebuild her confidence.
- **Journaling Her Achievements:** She started documenting her daily wins, big and small, to remind herself of her capabilities.
- **Exploring New Hobbies:** Emily joined a pottery class, rediscovering her creative side and making supportive friends.

The Transformation

Today, Emily runs her own successful design agency. Reflecting on her journey, she shares: "I've learned that my worth isn't tied to someone else's approval. I am proud of who I am, flaws and all."

2. David's Story: Reclaiming Independence from a Toxic Workplace
The Challenge

David, a 29-year-old software engineer, worked under a manager who constantly shifted blame onto him for team failures. Gaslighting phrases like "I never told you to do that" and "You're just not detail-oriented enough" left David doubting his skills.

The Turning Point

During a team meeting, a colleague privately messaged David to say, "I see the hard work you're putting in—it's not your fault the project went sideways." This moment of solidarity helped David see the toxic environment for what it was.

The Recovery

David took proactive steps to rebuild his professional confidence:

- **Documenting Evidence:** He kept detailed records of emails and project updates to counter his manager's claims.
- **Networking:** David connected with professionals outside his workplace, seeking advice and mentorship.
- **Job Hunting:** Armed with a strong portfolio and renewed confidence, he secured a position at a supportive, collaborative company.

The Transformation

In his new role, David thrives as a team leader. "Leaving that toxic environment was the best decision I ever made," he says. "Now, I'm in a place where my contributions are valued."

3. Sofia's Story: Rebuilding After an Emotionally Abusive Marriage

The Challenge

Sofia, a 42-year-old teacher, spent over a decade in a marriage where her husband controlled every aspect of her life. He gaslighted her into believing she was too emotional, too demanding, and too dependent to survive on her own.

The Turning Point

One day, Sofia overheard her young daughter apologizing excessively to a classmate, mirroring Sofia's own behavior. This moment became a wake-up call—she wanted to model strength and self-respect for her children.

The Recovery

Sofia's journey to freedom included:

- **Building a Safety Net:** She confided in close friends and family, who supported her in leaving the marriage.
- **Rediscovering Her Passions:** Sofia joined a local book club and started writing poetry, reconnecting with her creative side.
- **Practicing Self-Compassion:** Through therapy, she learned to replace self-criticism with kindness.

The Transformation

Today, Sofia is an advocate for survivors of emotional abuse. She reflects, "Leaving was terrifying, but it was also the start of a beautiful new chapter. I'm teaching my children—and myself—that we all deserve respect."

4. Liam's Story: Overcoming Gaslighting in a Family Dynamic

The Challenge

Liam, a 25-year-old college student, grew up with parents who frequently dismissed his emotions and decisions. "You're just being dramatic" and "You'll never succeed without our help" were common refrains, leaving him feeling powerless and dependent.

The Turning Point

While attending a campus workshop on emotional abuse, Liam recognized the gaslighting patterns in his family. This realization gave him the clarity to start setting boundaries.

The Recovery

Liam focused on regaining control over his life:

- **Therapy:** Working with a counselor, he learned to validate his own feelings and assert his needs.
- **Setting Boundaries:** He limited conversations with his parents to neutral topics and moved out of their home to reduce their influence.
- **Finding Supportive Connections:** Liam joined a student organization where he formed meaningful friendships.

The Transformation

Liam is now pursuing a graduate degree in psychology, inspired by his own journey. "I've learned that my worth isn't defined by others," he says. "I have the power to create my own path."

5. Mia's Story: Rediscovering Her Voice After Workplace Gaslighting

The Challenge

Mia, a 38-year-old marketing executive, endured years of subtle but persistent gaslighting from a senior colleague. Comments like "You're too sensitive to handle leadership" undermined her confidence and kept her from applying for promotions.

The Turning Point

During a professional development seminar, Mia met a mentor who encouraged her to challenge the narratives that had been imposed on her. This was the spark she needed to reclaim her ambitions.

The Recovery

Mia rebuilt her confidence step by step:

- **Professional Coaching:** She worked with a career coach to refine her skills and develop a leadership mindset.

- **Advocating for Herself:** Mia began speaking up in meetings and taking ownership of her ideas.
- **Building Allies:** She cultivated supportive relationships within her workplace, gaining allies who championed her capabilities.

The Transformation

Mia now leads a successful marketing team and mentors others facing workplace challenges. She reflects, "I almost believed I wasn't good enough. Now I know my voice matters, and I use it to uplift others."

Lessons from These Stories

1. **Awareness is the First Step:** Recognizing manipulation and its impact empowers you to take action.
2. **Support is Essential:** Whether from friends, family, colleagues, or professionals, a strong support network is invaluable for recovery.
3. **Healing Takes Time:** Each step, no matter how small, contributes to long-term growth and transformation.
4. **Empowerment is Possible:** Every survivor has the potential to reclaim their voice, rediscover their worth, and thrive.

Chapter 8: Living Gaslight-Free: Maintaining Healthy Relationships

Breaking free from gaslighting is a significant milestone, but maintaining a gaslight-free life requires learning to cultivate and sustain healthy, supportive relationships. In this chapter, we'll explore the hallmarks of positive relationships, strategies for fostering mutual respect, and techniques for safeguarding your emotional well-being. By building connections rooted in trust and understanding, you can create a fulfilling and emotionally safe environment.

---

1. Understanding the Hallmarks of Healthy Relationships

Key Traits of Positive Relationships

1. **Mutual Respect:** Both parties honor each other's boundaries, feelings, and opinions.
2. **Open Communication:** Conversations are honest, transparent, and judgment-free.
3. **Empathy and Support:** Partners, friends, or colleagues show understanding and provide encouragement during challenges.
4. **Equality:** Power dynamics are balanced, with no one dominating or controlling the other.
5. **Accountability:** Both parties take responsibility for their actions and address conflicts constructively.

Reflection Exercise:
Ask yourself:

- Do I feel heard and valued in my relationships?
- Are my needs and boundaries respected?
- Do these connections make me feel supported and safe?

2. Recognizing Red Flags in New Relationships

To maintain a gaslight-free life, it's essential to spot early signs of potential manipulation or toxicity.

Red Flags to Watch For:

- **Frequent Criticism:** They undermine your confidence with constant negative feedback.
- **Dismissiveness:** They belittle or invalidate your thoughts and emotions.
- **Control:** They attempt to dictate your choices, time, or interactions with others.
- **Excessive Flattery or Love-Bombing:** Overwhelming attention can mask manipulative intentions.
- **Reluctance to Take Responsibility:** They deflect blame or refuse to apologize for mistakes.

Tip: Trust your instincts. If something feels off, don't dismiss your concerns.

3. Setting Boundaries as a Foundation for Healthy Relationships

Boundaries are crucial for protecting your emotional well-being and ensuring mutual respect.

How to Set Boundaries:

1. **Identify Your Limits:** Reflect on what behaviors make you feel uncomfortable or drained.
    - **Example:** "I need uninterrupted time for myself after work."
2. **Communicate Clearly:** Express your boundaries assertively but respectfully.
    - **Example:** "I appreciate your input, but I prefer making decisions about my career independently."
3. **Enforce Consequences:** Consistently address boundary violations to reinforce their importance.
    - **Example:** "If you continue to criticize my choices, I'll end the conversation."

Boundary Affirmation:
"My boundaries are not selfish; they're an essential part of maintaining healthy relationships."

4. Building Strong Communication Skills

Healthy relationships thrive on clear and respectful communication.

Techniques for Effective Communication:

- **Active Listening:** Focus fully on what the other person is saying without interrupting.
    - **Response Example:** "I hear that you're feeling frustrated. Can we work through this together?"

- **"I" Statements:** Express your feelings and needs without blaming.
  - **Example:** "I feel overwhelmed when I'm interrupted. Can we agree to take turns speaking?"
- **Clarify Assumptions:** Ask questions to ensure mutual understanding.
  - **Example:** "Can you clarify what you mean by that? I want to make sure I understand."

Conflict Resolution Tips:

- Address issues calmly and directly.
- Avoid accusatory language, focusing instead on solutions.
- Agree to revisit the conversation if emotions escalate.

Outcome: Strong communication fosters trust, reduces misunderstandings, and resolves conflicts constructively.

5. Fostering Empathy and Emotional Support

Empathy is the cornerstone of supportive relationships. Cultivating emotional awareness helps deepen connections and foster understanding.

Empathy-Building Exercises:

- **Perspective-Taking:** Put yourself in the other person's shoes.
  - **Prompt:** "How might they be feeling, and why?"

- **Validating Emotions:** Acknowledge and affirm their feelings, even if you don't fully agree.
    - **Response Example:** "I understand why this is upsetting for you."
- **Offering Support:** Ask how you can help.
    - **Question Example:** "What can I do to support you in this situation?"

Empathy Reminder:
"Everyone's experience is unique, and understanding their perspective helps strengthen our connection."

6. Practicing Self-Awareness in Relationships

Healthy relationships begin with a healthy relationship with yourself.

Self-Awareness Practices:

1. **Reflect on Your Behavior:**
    - Ask yourself, "Am I communicating respectfully and openly?"
    - Recognize patterns where you might project insecurities or overstep boundaries.
2. **Own Your Mistakes:**
    - Acknowledge when you've made an error and apologize sincerely.
    - *Example:* "I'm sorry for interrupting you earlier. It wasn't fair to you."
3. **Recognize Your Needs:**
    - Regularly check in with yourself to ensure your relationships align with your values.

Outcome: Increased self-awareness leads to stronger, more balanced connections.

7. Building a Network of Positive Relationships

Surrounding yourself with supportive people helps create a nurturing and fulfilling social environment.

How to Build a Positive Network:

- **Seek Like-Minded Individuals:** Join groups, classes, or communities that align with your interests and values.
- **Prioritize Quality Over Quantity:** Focus on deepening meaningful relationships rather than maintaining many superficial ones.
- **Be a Positive Influence:** Show kindness, empathy, and respect to attract similar qualities in others.

Tip: Evaluate your social circle regularly, letting go of toxic relationships that drain your energy.

8. Maintaining Healthy Relationships Over Time

Long-lasting relationships require effort and intentionality to grow and thrive.

Tips for Sustaining Positive Connections:

- **Express Gratitude:** Regularly thank those in your life for their support and presence.
    - **Example:** "I really appreciate how you've been there for me. It means a lot."

- **Spend Quality Time:** Dedicate time to nurture your connections, whether through shared activities or deep conversations.
- **Adapt to Change:** Accept that relationships evolve and find ways to navigate transitions together.

Check-In Practice:
Schedule periodic check-ins to discuss how each of you feels about the relationship and address any concerns.

9. Redefining Your Relationship Standards

After experiencing gaslighting, it's essential to set higher standards for future relationships.

Creating a Relationship Manifesto:

1. **Define Your Must-Haves:**
   - **Examples:** "Respect for my boundaries, open communication, emotional support."
2. **List Your Deal-Breakers:**
   - **Examples:** "Manipulation, lack of accountability, chronic negativity."
3. **Write a Commitment to Yourself:**
   - **Example:** "I commit to prioritizing my emotional well-being and only investing in relationships that uplift and respect me."

A Guide to Recognizing Healthy Relationship Dynamics

Healthy relationships are essential for emotional well-being, personal growth, and overall life satisfaction. Whether the relationship is romantic, familial, platonic, or professional, certain dynamics consistently characterize positive, supportive connections. This guide will help you identify the signs of healthy relationships, offering practical insights into what to look for and how to cultivate these qualities in your interactions.

1. Hallmarks of Healthy Relationships
1.1 Mutual Respect

- **What It Looks Like:**
    - Both individuals value and honor each other's opinions, feelings, and boundaries.
    - Criticism is constructive, never demeaning or intended to undermine confidence.
    - Differences in perspective are accepted, not ridiculed or dismissed.
- **Example:** "I understand your viewpoint, even though I don't fully agree. Let's find a way to meet in the middle."

1.2 Open and Honest Communication

- **What It Looks Like:**
    - Both individuals feel safe expressing their thoughts and emotions without fear of judgment.
    - Transparency about feelings, intentions, and expectations reduces misunderstandings.

- Active listening—giving full attention and responding thoughtfully—is a priority.
- **Example:** "When you said that earlier, it hurt my feelings. Can we talk about it?"

1.3 Empathy and Understanding

- **What It Looks Like:**
    - Efforts are made to understand and validate each other's emotions, even if they differ.
    - Compassion replaces defensiveness or blame during disagreements.
    - Both parties strive to support each other during challenging times.
- **Example:** "I can see how that situation made you anxious. What can I do to help?"

1.4 Trust and Reliability

- **What It Looks Like:**
    - Promises are kept, and actions align with words.
    - There's confidence in the other person's intentions, without the need for constant reassurance.
    - Transparency fosters a sense of security, eliminating suspicion or doubt.
- **Example:** "I trust you to handle this, and I'll support whatever decision you make."

1.5 Healthy Boundaries

- **What It Looks Like:**

- Each person respects the other's personal space, time, and individual needs.
        - There's no pressure to compromise values or priorities for the relationship.
        - Boundaries are expressed clearly and honored without resistance.
- **Example:** "I need some quiet time after work. Let's catch up later this evening."

1.6 Shared Accountability

- **What It Looks Like:**
    - Both parties take responsibility for their actions and contributions to the relationship.
    - Mistakes are acknowledged, and apologies are sincere.
    - There's a commitment to resolving conflicts constructively.
- **Example:** "I'm sorry I overreacted earlier. Let's talk about how we can approach this better."

2. Practical Tools for Evaluating Relationship Dynamics
2.1 The Relationship Health Checklist

- Ask yourself:
    - Do I feel valued and respected in this relationship?
    - Is communication open, honest, and free of judgment?
    - Do I trust this person, and do they trust me?
    - Are my boundaries acknowledged and respected?

- Do we resolve conflicts collaboratively without resorting to blame or manipulation?

2.2 The "Energy Audit" Exercise

- Reflect on how you feel after interacting with someone:
  - **Energized and Positive:** Likely indicative of a healthy relationship.
  - **Drained or Anxious:** May signal unhealthy dynamics that need addressing.

3. Recognizing the Absence of Toxic Traits

Healthy relationships are often defined not just by the presence of positive qualities but also by the absence of toxic behaviors.

3.1 What Healthy Relationships Avoid:

- **Manipulation:** There's no use of guilt, fear, or deceit to control or influence behavior.
- **Gaslighting:** Emotions, memories, or experiences are never dismissed or distorted.
- **Codependency:** Both parties maintain their independence and sense of self.
- **Excessive Criticism:** Feedback is constructive, not used to demean or belittle.
- **Control:** Decisions are made collaboratively, not dictated by one person.

4. Examples of Healthy Relationship Dynamics
Romantic Relationship:

- **Scenario:** Jamie and Alex disagree on how to spend their weekend.
    - Jamie: "I was hoping for a quiet weekend at home."
    - Alex: "I'd like to go out with friends, but I understand you need time to recharge. How about we stay in Friday and go out Saturday?"
- **Why It's Healthy:** There's mutual understanding, respect for preferences, and a willingness to compromise.

Friendship:

- **Scenario:** Taylor feels overwhelmed and cancels plans with Sam at the last minute.
    - Sam: "I'm here if you need anything. Let's reschedule when you're feeling better."
- **Why It's Healthy:** Sam respects Taylor's need for space and offers support without resentment.

Workplace Relationship:

- **Scenario:** A colleague points out a mistake in your report.
    - Colleague: "I noticed a small error in your report. I know you've been juggling a lot—would you like help reviewing it?"
- **Why It's Healthy:** Feedback is delivered constructively, with an offer of support.

5. Cultivating and Sustaining Healthy Relationships
5.1 Prioritize Emotional Safety

- Foster an environment where both parties feel secure expressing their thoughts and emotions.
- Avoid judgment or ridicule, and offer encouragement instead.

5.2 Invest in Communication Skills

- Practice active listening, clarify misunderstandings, and express yourself with "I" statements.

5.3 Be Intentional About Time Together

- Dedicate quality time to deepen your connection, whether through shared activities, meaningful conversations, or simple gestures of appreciation.

5.4 Embrace Change and Growth

- Accept that relationships evolve and grow as individuals change.
- Approach these transitions with adaptability and a shared commitment to maintaining the connection.

6. Seeking Help When Needed

Even healthy relationships face challenges. Seeking professional guidance can help strengthen your bond and address underlying issues.

When to Seek Support:

- Persistent conflicts that seem unresolvable.
- Struggles with communication or unmet needs.
- Desire to strengthen the relationship and build deeper understanding.

Resources:

- Relationship counselors or therapists.
- Books and workshops on effective communication and emotional intelligence.

Tips on Fostering Open Communication and Trust

Open communication and trust are the cornerstones of healthy relationships. Whether in personal or professional contexts, these elements create a foundation for mutual respect, understanding, and emotional safety. Fostering these qualities requires intentional effort, self-awareness, and consistent practice. This guide provides actionable tips to help you cultivate open communication and build trust in any relationship.

1. Create a Safe Environment for Dialogue
Why It's Important:

People are more likely to communicate openly when they feel safe from judgment, criticism, or hostility.

How to Do It:

- **Be Approachable:** Maintain a calm and open demeanor. Avoid reacting defensively or dismissively.
    - **Example:** Instead of interrupting, nod or say, "I see what you mean. Tell me more."
- **Encourage Honesty:** Reassure the other person that their feelings and thoughts are valid, even if they differ from yours.
    - **Example:** "It's okay to feel that way. I appreciate you sharing it with me."
- **Practice Emotional Regulation:** Stay composed, even if the topic is sensitive or triggering.
    - **Tip:** Take deep breaths or suggest a pause if emotions escalate.

2. Practice Active Listening

Why It's Important:

Listening attentively fosters mutual respect and ensures that both parties feel heard and valued.

How to Do It:

- **Give Full Attention:** Put away distractions like phones or laptops during conversations.
    - **Tip:** Make eye contact and use affirming gestures like nodding.
- **Reflect Back:** Paraphrase what the other person says to confirm understanding.
    - **Example:** "So, you're saying you felt overlooked during the meeting. Is that correct?"

- **Ask Clarifying Questions:** Show genuine curiosity about their perspective.
  - **Example:** "Can you explain what you meant by that? I want to make sure I understand."

3. Be Transparent and Authentic
Why It's Important:

Transparency builds trust by demonstrating honesty and reliability.

How to Do It:

- **Share Your Feelings:** Express your emotions and thoughts openly, using "I" statements.
  - **Example:** "I felt hurt when our plans changed last minute. Can we talk about it?"
- **Be Honest About Limitations:** Admit when you don't know something or can't meet an expectation.
  - **Example:** "I can't take on this task right now, but I can help you find someone who can."
- **Avoid Hidden Agendas:** Be clear about your intentions to prevent misunderstandings.
  - **Example:** "I want to discuss this because I value our relationship and want to resolve any tension."

4. Build Consistency and Reliability
Why It's Important:

Trust grows when actions consistently align with words.

How to Do It:

- **Keep Promises:** Follow through on commitments, big or small.
    - **Example:** If you promise to call at a certain time, make sure you do.
- **Acknowledge Mistakes:** Take responsibility for errors and apologize sincerely.
    - **Example:** "I'm sorry I forgot our meeting. I'll set a reminder next time to make sure it doesn't happen again."
- **Demonstrate Accountability:** Own your part in conflicts and work toward solutions.
    - **Example:** "I realize I didn't communicate clearly. Let's work together to fix this."

5. Encourage Two-Way Communication
Why It's Important:

Healthy relationships are built on balanced exchanges where both parties feel equally valued.

How to Do It:

- **Invite Feedback:** Ask for input and be open to constructive criticism.
    - **Example:** "How do you feel about how we handled that situation? Is there anything I could have done differently?"
- **Share Decision-Making:** Collaborate on choices rather than dictating outcomes.

- **Example:** "What do you think is the best way to approach this? Let's decide together."
- **Validate Their Perspective:** Even if you disagree, acknowledge their right to feel or think a certain way.
  - **Example:** "I see why you feel that way, and I respect your opinion."

6. Address Conflicts Constructively
Why It's Important:

How you handle disagreements can either strengthen or damage trust.

How to Do It:

- **Stay Solution-Focused:** Shift the conversation from blame to resolution.
  - **Example**: "How can we work together to prevent this issue in the future?"
- **Avoid Personal Attacks:** Critique behaviors, not character.
  - **Example:** Instead of saying, "You're so careless," say, "I felt frustrated when the project was delayed."
- **Take Breaks if Needed:** Pause heated discussions to prevent escalation.
  - **Example:** "Let's take a break and come back to this with a clear head."

7. Respect Boundaries
Why It's Important:

Honoring boundaries shows that you respect the other person's needs and autonomy.

How to Do It:

- **Ask About Preferences:** Learn what makes the other person comfortable or uncomfortable.
    - **Example:** "Do you prefer discussing this now or later?"
- **Accept "No" Gracefully:** Respect their decision without pushing.
    - **Example:** "I understand you're not ready to talk. Let me know when you are."
- **Set Your Own Boundaries:** Clearly communicate your limits and enforce them consistently.
    - **Example:** "I'm not comfortable discussing this over text. Can we talk in person?"

8. Foster Empathy and Understanding
Why It's Important:

Empathy deepens emotional connections and builds trust by showing genuine care.

How to Do It:

- **Acknowledge Their Emotions:** Validate feelings, even if you don't share them.

- **Example:** "That sounds really tough. I'm sorry you're going through this."
- **Be Patient:** Give them time to articulate their thoughts or process their emotions.
- **Put Yourself in Their Shoes:** Try to see the situation from their perspective.
  - **Example:** "If I were in your position, I'd probably feel the same way."

9. Cultivate a Growth Mindset in Relationships
Why It's Important:

A willingness to learn and adapt strengthens relationships and builds trust over time.

How to Do It:

- **Learn from Mistakes:** View conflicts as opportunities to grow and improve.
  - **Example:** "I've realized that I wasn't as supportive as I could have been. I'll do better moving forward."
- **Celebrate Progress:** Acknowledge positive changes and efforts in the relationship.
  - **Example:** "I appreciate how we've been communicating more openly lately."
- **Be Open to Change:** Adapt to evolving dynamics and find ways to strengthen your bond.

10. Use Technology to Enhance Communication (Not Replace It)

Why It's Important:

While technology can facilitate communication, it's no substitute for meaningful, face-to-face interactions.

How to Do It:

- **Use Technology Thoughtfully:** Send texts or emails for logistics but prioritize in-person or video conversations for emotional discussions.
- **Avoid Misinterpretations:** Clarify tone and intent when communicating digitally.
    - **Example:** "Just to clarify, I meant that as a joke—I hope it didn't come across otherwise."
- **Set Tech Boundaries:** Agree on times to disconnect and focus on each other.
    - **Example:** "Let's put our phones away during dinner."

Checklist for Identifying Supportive People and Potential Red Flags in New Relationships

Forming new relationships—whether romantic, platonic, or professional—can be exciting but also challenging. It's essential to identify supportive people while staying alert to potential red flags that might indicate unhealthy dynamics. This checklist will help you evaluate new relationships, ensuring they contribute positively to your well-being.

Part 1: Characteristics of Supportive People

Supportive individuals foster mutual respect, understanding, and growth. Use this checklist to identify these positive traits in new relationships.

1. Communication

- ☐ They listen actively and give you their full attention.
- ☐ They express themselves honestly and transparently.
- ☐ They respect your opinions, even if they disagree.
- ☐ They ask questions to better understand your thoughts and feelings.

2. Respect for Boundaries

- ☐ They respect your personal space, time, and decisions.
- ☐ They don't pressure you to do things you're uncomfortable with.
- ☐ They honor your "no" without pushing back or guilt-tripping.
- ☐ They check in to ensure you're comfortable during interactions.

3. Empathy and Emotional Support

- ☐ They validate your feelings without dismissing or minimizing them.
- ☐ They offer support during difficult times without making it about themselves.
- ☐ They show genuine interest in your well-being and happiness.
- ☐ They celebrate your achievements without jealousy or resentment.

4. Trust and Reliability

- ☐ They follow through on promises and commitments.
- ☐ They are honest about their intentions and actions.
- ☐ They handle conflicts calmly and constructively.
- ☐ They respect your privacy and don't share your personal information without consent.

5. Encouragement and Growth

- ☐ They encourage you to pursue your goals and passions.
- ☐ They offer constructive feedback without being critical or harsh.
- ☐ They are happy to see you grow, even if it means changes in the relationship.

- ☐ They support your independence and autonomy.

Part 2: Red Flags to Watch For

Unhealthy relationships often involve patterns of manipulation, disrespect, or control. This checklist outlines red flags that may indicate a potentially toxic dynamic.

1. Communication Issues

- ☐ They frequently interrupt or talk over you.
- ☐ They dismiss your thoughts or feelings as unimportant or irrational.
- ☐ They are overly critical or use sarcasm to undermine you.
- ☐ They refuse to engage in open or meaningful conversations.

2. Boundary Violations

- ☐ They ignore or push against boundaries you've set.
- ☐ They invade your privacy by snooping through your personal belongings or devices.
- ☐ They pressure you into making decisions or doing things you're uncomfortable with.
- ☐ They demand constant access to your time or attention.

3. Manipulative Behaviors

- ☐ They use guilt, fear, or flattery to influence your decisions.
- ☐ They frequently shift blame onto you during conflicts.
- ☐ They deny or distort past conversations or events to make you doubt yourself.
- ☐ They exhibit controlling behaviors, such as monitoring your activities or isolating you from others.

4. Emotional Instability

- ☐ They have unpredictable mood swings that impact your interactions.
- ☐ They become overly dependent on you for emotional support.
- ☐ They react defensively or explosively to minor disagreements.
- ☐ They use emotional outbursts to manipulate or intimidate you.

5. Disrespect and Dishonesty

- ☐ They frequently lie or withhold important information.
- ☐ They make fun of or belittle your beliefs, preferences, or goals.

- ☐ They treat you or others poorly, such as being rude to service workers.
- ☐ They show signs of jealousy or resentment over your achievements or other relationships.

Part 3: Practical Exercises for Evaluation
1. Reflect on Interactions

After spending time with someone new, ask yourself:

- Did I feel heard and respected?
- Did I feel comfortable being myself around them?
- Did the interaction leave me feeling positive and energized, or drained and uneasy?

2. Test Boundaries

Set a small boundary early in the relationship and observe their response:

- **Example:** Say you can't attend a social event or need alone time.
    - Supportive Response: "That's okay! Let me know if you change your mind."
    - Red Flag Response: "Why don't you want to come? Don't you care about me?"

3. Check Consistency

Pay attention to whether their words align with their actions:

- Do they keep promises and follow through on commitments?
- Are their behaviors consistent across different settings and with different people?

4. Observe Their Relationships with Others

How they treat friends, family, or colleagues can reveal their character:

- Do they speak respectfully about others?
- Do they maintain healthy boundaries and balanced dynamics?

Part 4: Cultivating Supportive Relationships
1. Focus on Mutual Effort

Healthy relationships require effort from both parties. Ensure that the dynamic is balanced and reciprocal.

2. Communicate Your Needs

Be clear about your expectations and boundaries from the beginning:

- **Example:** "It's important to me that we can both express ourselves openly and respect each other's time."

3. Trust Your Intuition

If something feels off, don't ignore it. Take time to assess the situation and prioritize your emotional well-being.

4. Seek Feedback

Ask trusted friends or family for their perspective on the new relationship. They may notice red flags or positive traits you've overlooked.

Chapter 9: The Role of Society: Gaslighting in Media and Culture

Gaslighting, while often associated with personal relationships, extends far beyond the individual sphere. It infiltrates media, cultural norms, and societal structures, shaping perceptions of reality on a collective scale. This chapter explores how gaslighting manifests in media and culture, its impact on society, and ways to recognize and resist these manipulative tactics.

1. Understanding Societal Gaslighting
What Is Societal Gaslighting?

Societal gaslighting occurs when institutions, media outlets, or cultural narratives manipulate public perceptions, distort facts, or delegitimize individual and collective experiences. This can reinforce power imbalances, marginalize certain groups, and perpetuate harmful ideologies.

Examples of Societal Gaslighting:

- Denying systemic issues, such as racism or sexism, by reframing them as isolated incidents or exaggerations.
- Portraying victims of abuse as overly sensitive or fabricating their experiences.
- Using media to present biased narratives that dismiss valid dissent or criticism.

Key Question:
How do societal narratives shape what we perceive as truth or reality?

2. Gaslighting in Media
2.1 Manipulation Through News and Journalism

The media plays a significant role in shaping public opinion. When used unethically, it can manipulate facts and foster societal gaslighting.

- **Selective Reporting:** Highlighting certain events while ignoring others creates a skewed perspective.
  - **Example:** Overemphasizing violent protests while underreporting peaceful demonstrations to delegitimize social movements.
- **Repetition of Falsehoods:** Repeating untruths can make them seem credible, a phenomenon known as the "illusory truth effect."
  - **Example**: Constantly asserting that climate change is a hoax, despite overwhelming scientific evidence.

2.2 The Role of Social Media

Social media amplifies societal gaslighting by spreading misinformation and fostering echo chambers.

- **Algorithms and Bias:** Platforms prioritize sensationalist content, reinforcing pre-existing beliefs and dismissing alternative perspectives.
- **Cancel Culture:** Mischaracterizing individuals or groups without context can distort public perceptions and suppress dialogue.

How to Recognize Media Gaslighting:

- Analyze the language used—does it aim to provoke fear or doubt?
- Seek out multiple sources to cross-check facts.
- Be cautious of headlines that oversimplify complex issues.

3. Cultural Narratives as Tools of Gaslighting
3.1 Marginalization Through Stereotypes

Cultural narratives often reinforce harmful stereotypes that invalidate the experiences of marginalized groups.

- **Examples:**
    - Labeling women who advocate for equal rights as "hysterical" or "man-hating."
    - Portraying racial minorities as perpetually disadvantaged or undeserving of opportunities.
    - Framing mental health struggles as weakness rather than legitimate concerns.

3.2 Erasure of Historical Truths

- **What It Is:** Downplaying or rewriting historical events to benefit dominant groups.
    - **Example**: Minimizing the impact of colonialism or slavery in school curricula.
- **Impact:** This erasure delegitimizes the experiences of affected communities, fostering collective doubt and disengagement.

4. Gaslighting in Advertising and Consumer Culture
4.1 Emotional Manipulation

Advertising often exploits insecurities to promote products as solutions to nonexistent problems.

- **Examples:**
    - Promoting unattainable beauty standards, making individuals feel inadequate.
    - Selling products by implying they're essential for social acceptance or happiness.

4.2 Greenwashing and Misinformation

Corporations use gaslighting tactics to appear environmentally friendly or socially responsible while engaging in harmful practices.

- **Examples:**
    - Claiming to use "sustainable" practices without providing verifiable proof.
    - Highlighting token charitable efforts while ignoring significant ethical violations.

5. Political Gaslighting and Its Societal Impact
5.1 Denial of Evidence

Political leaders often use gaslighting to dismiss or distort facts, undermining trust in experts and institutions.

- **Examples:**

- Denying the existence of systemic inequalities despite statistical evidence.
- Reframing protests against injustice as attacks on societal stability.

5.2 Polarization Through False Narratives

Divisive rhetoric pits groups against each other, making collective action difficult.

- **Impact:**
    - Distracts from systemic issues by encouraging infighting among the public.
    - Creates a false sense of security for those benefiting from the status quo.

6. Recognizing and Resisting Societal Gaslighting
6.1 Critical Thinking Skills

- Question dominant narratives and consider whose interests they serve.
- Evaluate evidence critically, distinguishing between opinion and fact.

6.2 Amplify Marginalized Voices

- Support platforms and individuals that challenge mainstream narratives.
- Share stories that provide context and highlight lived experiences.

6.3 Advocate for Media Literacy

- Educate yourself and others on how to identify bias, misinformation, and manipulation in media.
- Encourage schools and communities to adopt media literacy programs.

6.4 Demand Accountability

- Hold institutions, corporations, and media outlets accountable for dishonest practices.
- Support independent journalism and organizations committed to transparency.

7. The Role of Individuals in Shaping a Gaslight-Free Society
7.1 Cultivate Awareness

- Recognize your biases and how societal narratives may influence your perceptions.
- Stay informed by seeking diverse perspectives and engaging in meaningful dialogue.

7.2 Build Inclusive Communities

- Foster environments where all voices are valued and respected.
- Challenge stereotypes and prejudices when they arise in conversations or media.

7.3 Empower Others

- Support initiatives that empower marginalized groups to share their stories.
- Advocate for systemic changes that promote equity and justice.

Analysis of Gaslighting in Advertising, Politics, and Pop Culture

Gaslighting—a psychological manipulation technique that distorts reality—extends beyond personal relationships and is often wielded as a tool of influence in advertising, politics, and pop culture. These spheres exploit gaslighting tactics to shape public perception, control narratives, and drive consumer or voter behavior. This chapter analyzes how gaslighting manifests in these domains and its far-reaching consequences.

1. Gaslighting in Advertising

Advertising leverages gaslighting to manipulate emotions, exploit insecurities, and create artificial needs. This form of psychological manipulation often distorts reality to influence consumer behavior.

1.1 Creating Insecurities

Advertising frequently preys on people's vulnerabilities by implying they are incomplete or inadequate without certain products.

- **Examples:**

- **Beauty Standards:** Ads promoting flawless skin, thin bodies, or perfect hair imply that anything less is undesirable.
    - **Message:** "You're not enough as you are; you need this product to be attractive."
- **Lifestyle Expectations:** Luxury brands suggest that wealth or specific possessions equate to happiness and social status.
    - **Message:** "If you don't own this, you're failing at life."

1.2 Reinforcing Unattainable Ideals

Advertisers present unrealistic images of beauty, success, or happiness, creating a cycle of dissatisfaction.

- **Example:** Airbrushed models in skincare ads are portrayed as the norm, making consumers feel inadequate and desperate for solutions.

1.3 False Claims and Greenwashing

Brands use misleading statements to manipulate consumer perception, often portraying themselves as more ethical or environmentally friendly than they are.

- **Examples:**
    - Products labeled "natural" or "eco-friendly" with no verifiable standards.
    - Companies highlighting small charitable efforts while engaging in harmful practices behind the scenes.

Impact of Advertising Gaslighting:

- Distorted self-image and increased consumer anxiety.
- Perpetuation of societal inequalities, such as classism or sexism.
- Overconsumption driven by a manufactured sense of inadequacy.

2. Gaslighting in Politics

In politics, gaslighting is a powerful tool for controlling narratives, dismissing dissent, and influencing public opinion. Politicians and institutions use these tactics to obscure truth, sow confusion, and maintain power.

2.1 Denying Reality

Politicians frequently gaslight by denying facts or evidence that contradict their agendas, making people question their perceptions.

- **Examples:**
    - Denying climate change despite overwhelming scientific evidence.
    - Downplaying systemic racism by reframing it as isolated incidents.

2.2 Rewriting History

Historical events are often distorted to fit political narratives, erasing inconvenient truths or reframing actions in a more favorable light.

- **Examples:**
    - Glossing over the negative impacts of colonialism in educational curricula.
    - Politicians claiming credit for successes they didn't achieve or blaming others for failures they caused.

2.3 Divisive Rhetoric

Gaslighting tactics are used to polarize society, pitting groups against each other to distract from systemic issues.

- **Examples:**
    - Portraying immigrants as threats to economic stability without addressing deeper economic inequities.
    - Rebranding protests as attacks on societal order rather than legitimate calls for change.

2.4 False Promises and Shifting Blame

Politicians often gaslight voters by making unattainable promises and redirecting blame when they fail to deliver.

- **Examples:**
    - Promising sweeping reforms without the means to achieve them.
    - Blaming external factors or political opponents for policy failures.

Impact of Political Gaslighting:

- Erosion of public trust in institutions and media.

- Increased division and misinformation within communities.
- Disempowerment of marginalized groups by invalidating their experiences and concerns.

3. Gaslighting in Pop Culture

Pop culture, encompassing movies, TV shows, music, and social media, plays a significant role in shaping societal norms and values. Gaslighting in pop culture can normalize harmful dynamics, distort historical truths, and perpetuate stereotypes.

3.1 Normalization of Toxic Relationships

Movies and TV shows often romanticize unhealthy dynamics, making manipulation appear acceptable or even desirable.

- **Examples:**
  - Romantic comedies where controlling or emotionally abusive behavior is framed as passionate love.
    - **Message:** "Jealousy and possessiveness are signs of deep affection."
  - TV dramas that glorify manipulation and deceit as signs of intelligence or power.

3.2 Reinforcing Harmful Stereotypes

Pop culture frequently perpetuates gaslighting by portraying marginalized groups through biased or one-dimensional lenses.

- **Examples:**
  - Depicting women as overly emotional or irrational, reinforcing the stereotype that their concerns are invalid.
  - Portraying racial minorities as inherently violent or uneducated, perpetuating systemic biases.

3.3 Historical Distortions

Movies and media often rewrite historical events to align with dominant narratives, erasing the contributions or suffering of marginalized groups.

- **Examples:**
  - Films glorifying colonialism while ignoring its devastating impacts on indigenous populations.
  - War movies that omit atrocities committed by the "heroic" side.

3.4 Social Media Amplification

Social media influencers and platforms use gaslighting tactics to manipulate followers, promote harmful trends, or distort reality.

- **Examples:**
  - Filters and editing tools that create unattainable beauty standards.
  - Viral challenges that downplay serious issues or promote risky behaviors.

Impact of Pop Culture Gaslighting:

- Perpetuation of toxic relationship dynamics and unrealistic expectations.
- Reinforcement of systemic biases and inequalities.
- Erosion of critical thinking due to the glamorization of manipulation.

4. How to Recognize and Resist Gaslighting in These Domains

4.1 Critical Thinking

- Question the motives behind advertisements, political statements, or media narratives.
- Research multiple sources to verify claims and seek alternative perspectives.

4.2 Media Literacy

- Learn to identify bias, sensationalism, and manipulation in media and pop culture.
- Teach others, especially younger audiences, to discern credible content from propaganda.

4.3 Advocate for Accountability

- Support organizations and initiatives that promote transparency in advertising, politics, and media.
- Demand ethical practices from brands, politicians, and content creators.

4.4 Celebrate Diverse Voices

- Amplify content from underrepresented communities to challenge dominant narratives.
- Support independent media and creators who prioritize authenticity and inclusivity.

Case Studies: How Societal Gaslighting Affects Marginalized Groups

Societal gaslighting manipulates collective narratives to distort the realities of marginalized groups, perpetuating systemic inequities and invalidating lived experiences. Through case studies, this chapter examines how societal gaslighting manifests and impacts various marginalized communities, exploring real-world examples and their far-reaching consequences.

Case Study 1: Denial of Systemic Racism
The Scenario:

In the aftermath of highly publicized incidents of police brutality, calls for racial justice surged across the globe. Movements like Black Lives Matter (BLM) highlighted systemic racism in policing, housing, healthcare, and education. However, societal gaslighting emerged as a significant obstacle to progress.

Manifestations of Societal Gaslighting:

- **Dismissal of Evidence:**

- Claims like "Racism isn't a problem anymore" or "All lives matter" were used to minimize the movement's focus on racial inequities.
- Data showing racial disparities in arrest rates, sentencing, and use of force were dismissed as exaggerated or fabricated.
- **Reframing Narratives:**
  - Peaceful protests were often portrayed as violent riots, undermining their legitimacy and deterring public support.
- **Blame Shifting:**
  - Critics blamed marginalized communities for their own struggles, perpetuating stereotypes of laziness or criminality.

Impact on Marginalized Communities:

- **Erosion of Trust:** Gaslighting narratives invalidated the experiences of people of color, eroding trust in institutions and allies.
- **Perpetuation of Stereotypes:** Media portrayal reinforced negative biases, further marginalizing affected groups.
- **Emotional Toll:** Constant denial of systemic racism caused collective frustration, exhaustion, and feelings of helplessness.

Insights:

Societal gaslighting around racism perpetuates inequity by silencing valid concerns, deterring systemic reform, and marginalizing voices calling for justice.

Case Study 2: Gaslighting Women in the Workplace
The Scenario:

Women navigating corporate environments frequently face societal gaslighting that undermines their credibility, capabilities, and rightful place in leadership roles.

Manifestations of Societal Gaslighting:

1. **Stereotyping and Dismissal:**
   - Women expressing ambition or confidence were labeled "bossy" or "too aggressive."
   - Concerns about workplace harassment were dismissed as "overreactions" or "misunderstandings."
2. **Unequal Standards:**
   - Women were held to higher standards than male counterparts, but their successes were often attributed to luck or favoritism.
3. **Rewriting Experiences:**
   - When reporting discrimination, women were told they were being overly emotional or imagining bias.

Impact on Women:

- **Career Stagnation:** Gaslighting discouraged women from pursuing leadership roles, fearing further invalidation or backlash.
- **Mental Health Challenges:** Experiencing persistent invalidation led to anxiety, self-doubt, and burnout.

- **Economic Disparities:** Lack of promotions and equal pay exacerbated gender wage gaps.

Insights:

Societal gaslighting in professional settings reinforces the glass ceiling, stifling gender equity and undermining progress toward workplace inclusivity.

Case Study 3: LGBTQ+ Community and Erasure of Identity
The Scenario:

LGBTQ+ individuals have long been subjected to societal gaslighting that delegitimizes their identities, experiences, and rights.

Manifestations of Societal Gaslighting:

1. **Invalidation of Identity:**
    - Trans individuals were told their gender identities were "just a phase" or not real.
    - Same-sex relationships were dismissed as "unnatural" or reduced to a lifestyle choice.
2. **Reframing Advocacy as Aggression:**
    - Calls for equal rights were reframed as attacks on "traditional values" or religious freedom.
3. **Minimization of Discrimination:**
    - Issues like hate crimes and workplace discrimination were downplayed, with narratives suggesting that LGBTQ+ individuals were exaggerating their challenges.

Impact on the LGBTQ+ Community:

- **Psychological Harm:** Gaslighting contributed to higher rates of depression, anxiety, and suicide within the LGBTQ+ population.
- **Social Isolation:** Individuals felt disconnected from their families, communities, and workplaces due to invalidation.
- **Barriers to Advocacy:** Societal narratives often undermined the urgency and legitimacy of LGBTQ+ rights movements.

Insights:

Societal gaslighting marginalizes LGBTQ+ voices, perpetuates stigma, and delays progress toward full equality and acceptance.

Case Study 4: The Environmental Justice Movement and Indigenous Communities

The Scenario:

Indigenous communities advocating for environmental justice face societal gaslighting that downplays the environmental degradation they experience and delegitimizes their activism.

Manifestations of Societal Gaslighting:

1. **Dismissal of Knowledge:**
    - Indigenous environmental knowledge was labeled as "unscientific" or irrelevant.
2. **Reframing Activism:**

- Activists opposing harmful industrial projects were painted as "anti-progress" or "troublemakers."
3. **Minimization of Harm:**
   - The impact of deforestation, mining, or oil drilling on Indigenous lands was dismissed as insignificant.

Impact on Indigenous Communities:

- **Loss of Cultural Heritage:** Gaslighting narratives facilitated the destruction of sacred sites and traditional ways of life.
- **Economic Disparities:** Environmental harm further entrenched poverty and inequity within Indigenous communities.
- **Erosion of Advocacy Efforts:** Public support for environmental justice movements waned due to distorted narratives.

Insights:

Societal gaslighting around environmental justice perpetuates ecological harm, disregards Indigenous voices, and delays necessary reforms.

Case Study 5: Mental Health Stigma
The Scenario:

Individuals seeking mental health support often face societal gaslighting that invalidates their struggles and discourages treatment.

Manifestations of Societal Gaslighting:

1. **Minimization of Symptoms:**
   - Mental health issues were dismissed as "just stress" or "all in your head."
2. **Stigma Around Help-Seeking:**
   - Therapy or medication was framed as a sign of weakness rather than strength.
3. **Reframing Mental Health Crises:**
   - Individuals experiencing crises were labeled as attention-seeking or dangerous, rather than in need of compassion.

Impact on People with Mental Health Challenges:

- **Delayed Treatment:** Fear of judgment prevented individuals from seeking help.
- **Internalized Stigma:** Gaslighting narratives led people to doubt their own experiences and worth.
- **Social Isolation:** Misunderstanding and invalidation from peers and family exacerbated feelings of loneliness.

Insights:

Societal gaslighting around mental health perpetuates stigma, hinders treatment, and undermines public understanding of psychological well-being.

Tips for Becoming More Media-Savvy and Critical of Manipulative Messaging

In today's world, where media is omnipresent, learning to navigate and critically assess manipulative messaging is a crucial skill. Advertising, social media, news outlets, and pop culture often employ subtle tactics to influence perceptions and behavior. By becoming more media-savvy, you can protect yourself from manipulation and make informed decisions. This guide offers practical tips to help you decode, analyze, and resist manipulative messaging in media.

1. Understand Common Manipulative Tactics

The first step to resisting manipulation is recognizing the techniques used to influence emotions and perceptions.

1.1 Emotional Appeals

- **What It Is:** Messages designed to evoke strong emotions such as fear, guilt, or happiness to sway opinions.
- **Examples:**
    - Fear-based political ads predicting dire consequences if an opponent is elected.
    - Charity campaigns that use images of suffering to elicit donations without explaining how funds are used.

1.2 False Dichotomies

- **What It Is:** Presenting two extreme choices while ignoring alternatives.

- **Examples:**
  - "You're either with us or against us."
  - "If you don't buy this product, you're falling behind."

1.3 Misinformation and Misrepresentation

- **What It Is:** Spreading false information or framing facts selectively to distort the truth.
- **Examples:**
  - Cherry-picking statistics to support a biased narrative.
  - Using edited photos or videos to mislead viewers.

1.4 Repetition

- **What It Is:** Repeating a claim so frequently that it starts to feel true (the "illusory truth effect").
- **Examples:**
  - Political slogans that oversimplify complex issues.
  - Persistent advertising claims like "#1 Brand Recommended by Experts" without evidence.

Action Tip: Create a list of these tactics and keep them in mind when consuming media.

2. Diversify Your Media Sources

Relying on a single source can expose you to bias and manipulative messaging. Diversifying your media consumption ensures a more balanced perspective.

How to Do It:

1. **Explore Different Outlets:**
   - Follow news from various ideological perspectives (e.g., left-leaning, right-leaning, independent).
   - Include international news to gain a broader context on global issues.
2. **Fact-Check Information:**
   - Use reliable fact-checking platforms like Snopes, PolitiFact, or FactCheck.org.
3. **Balance Formats:**
   - Read long-form journalism, listen to podcasts, and watch documentaries to gain deeper insights.

Action Tip: Regularly compare how different sources report the same event to identify potential biases or omissions.

3. Question the Source's Motives

Every media message has a purpose, whether to inform, entertain, sell, or persuade. Identifying the agenda behind the content helps you evaluate its credibility.

Questions to Ask:

- **Who created this content?**
  - Is it a reputable journalist, an influencer, a corporation, or an anonymous source?
- **What is their goal?**
  - Are they aiming to inform, sell a product, or promote a specific viewpoint?

- **Who benefits from this message?**
    - Is it the audience, the creator, or a third party (e.g., advertisers)?

Action Tip: Be cautious of content that prioritizes sensationalism over accuracy or transparency.

4. Develop Critical Thinking Skills

Approaching media with a critical mindset helps you analyze its content, context, and intent.

How to Develop Critical Thinking:

1. **Analyze the Language:**
    - Look for emotionally charged words, exaggerations, or absolutes like "always" or "never."
    - **Example:** "This product will change your life!" (Examine the claim critically.)
2. **Identify Logical Fallacies:**
    - Common fallacies include:
        - *Ad hominem:* Attacking a person instead of their argument.
        - *Appeal to authority:* Assuming something is true because an expert endorses it.
        - *Slippery slope:* Suggesting one action will inevitably lead to disastrous consequences.
3. **Evaluate the Evidence:**
    - Does the message cite credible sources or rely on anecdotes and vague statistics?

Action Tip: Use tools like the CRAAP Test (Currency, Relevance, Authority, Accuracy, Purpose) to assess the reliability of content.

5. Recognize Biases (Including Your Own)

Bias exists in all media—and in your perceptions. Acknowledging these biases helps you approach content objectively.

Types of Bias in Media:

- **Confirmation Bias:** Favoring information that aligns with your beliefs.
- **Selection Bias:** Highlighting specific facts while ignoring others.
- **Framing Bias:** Presenting information in a way that influences interpretation.

How to Mitigate Bias:

- Actively seek opposing viewpoints.
- Reflect on how your values and experiences might influence your interpretation.
- Be open to changing your perspective when presented with new evidence.

Action Tip: Regularly challenge your assumptions by engaging with diverse perspectives.

6. Examine Visual and Digital Cues

Images, videos, and digital content can subtly manipulate emotions and perceptions.

What to Look For:

- **Editing Techniques:** Cropped or edited photos and videos may misrepresent events.
- **Body Language and Tone:** In interviews or debates, observe how non-verbal cues influence your perception of the speaker.
- **Design Elements:** Bold fonts, bright colors, or dramatic music are often used to evoke emotions.

Action Tip: Use reverse image search tools (e.g., Google Lens) to verify the authenticity of visual content.

7. Resist Clickbait and Sensationalism

Clickbait headlines and sensationalist content are designed to grab attention, often at the expense of accuracy.

How to Resist:

- Read beyond the headline to understand the full story.
- Be skeptical of claims that seem too good (or bad) to be true.
- Cross-check facts with credible sources before sharing.

Action Tip: Pause and reflect before reacting to or sharing emotionally charged content.

8. Practice Digital Literacy

With the rise of misinformation online, digital literacy is essential for navigating the digital landscape effectively.

Key Digital Literacy Skills:

- **Evaluate Websites:**
    - Check the "About" section to understand the site's purpose and credibility.
- **Recognize Bots and Trolls:**
    - Be cautious of accounts with generic usernames, minimal activity, or excessive posting.
- **Understand Algorithms:**
    - Recognize that social media platforms prioritize engagement, not accuracy.

Action Tip: Use browser extensions or apps (e.g., NewsGuard) to evaluate the trustworthiness of websites.

9. Educate Yourself and Others

The more you learn about media manipulation, the better equipped you'll be to resist it—and to help others do the same.

How to Educate Yourself:

- Take online courses in media literacy or critical thinking.
- Read books and articles on propaganda, media ethics, and cognitive biases.

How to Educate Others:

- Share resources and tools with friends, family, or colleagues.
- Engage in respectful discussions about manipulative messaging and how to spot it.

Action Tip: Start by teaching younger audiences to critically evaluate media, as they are often more vulnerable to manipulation.

10. Take Breaks and Reflect

Constant exposure to media can make it harder to think critically. Regular breaks allow you to process information and reduce emotional reactivity.

How to Disconnect:

- Schedule "media-free" periods to focus on other activities.
- Use apps to limit time spent on social media or news platforms.

Action Tip: Reflect on how media consumption affects your emotions, behavior, and decision-making.

Chapter 10: Gaslighting Recovery Toolkit

Recovering from gaslighting is a transformative journey that requires healing, rebuilding self-esteem, and fostering self-empowerment. The effects of gaslighting—self-doubt, confusion, and a fractured sense of self—can linger long after the manipulative relationship ends. This chapter offers a **Gaslighting Recovery Toolkit**, packed with actionable strategies, exercises, and resources to support long-term recovery and empower you to thrive.

1. Rebuilding Self-Trust

Gaslighting erodes trust in your perceptions, memories, and decisions. Rebuilding self-trust is foundational to recovery.

1.1 Reality Validation

- **Tool:** Keep a "Reality Journal."
    - Write down daily events, how they made you feel, and any conflicts or doubts.
    - Revisit your entries regularly to affirm your perceptions and reflect on patterns.
    - **Example:** "I felt dismissed in a meeting. Reviewing this later, I see my perspective was valid, even if it wasn't acknowledged."

1.2 Decision-Making Practice

- **Exercise:** Start with small decisions, like choosing what to eat or wear.

- Gradually increase to more significant choices, such as setting boundaries or pursuing personal goals.
- Celebrate each decision to reinforce confidence in your judgment.

2. Reconnecting with Your Identity

Gaslighting often causes a loss of identity. Rediscovering who you are helps you rebuild your sense of self.

2.1 Self-Discovery Activities

- **Tool:** "Who Am I?" Exercise
    - Create lists answering:
        - What are my values?
        - What brings me joy?
        - What strengths have I demonstrated in tough situations?
    - Use these lists to guide decisions and set personal goals.

2.2 Vision Board

- Visualize your ideal future by creating a vision board with images, quotes, and goals.
- Reflect on it regularly to stay focused on your aspirations.

3. Healing Emotional Wounds

Emotional recovery involves processing pain and rebuilding resilience.

3.1 Emotional Processing

- **Tool:** Journaling
    - Write freely about your experiences, emotions, and thoughts without judgment.
    - Use prompts such as:
        - *What would I say to my past self?*
        - *What lessons have I learned from this experience?*

3.2 Practicing Self-Compassion

- Replace self-critical thoughts with compassionate statements:
    - *Instead of:* "I should have known better."
    - *Say:* "I did the best I could with the knowledge I had at the time."
- Use affirmations like:
    - "I deserve kindness and respect."
    - "I am enough, just as I am."

4. Setting Healthy Boundaries

Boundaries protect your emotional well-being and help prevent future manipulation.

4.1 Identifying Boundaries

- Reflect on past experiences to identify your limits:
    - **Example:** "I need alone time after work to recharge."

- Write down non-negotiable boundaries for relationships, work, and self-care.

4.2 Communicating Boundaries

- Use clear, assertive language:
    - **Example:** "I'm not comfortable discussing that topic. Let's focus on something else."
- Practice saying "no" without guilt:
    - **Example:** "I can't take on that project right now."

5. Building Supportive Relationships

Surrounding yourself with supportive people fosters a nurturing environment for recovery.

5.1 Identifying Supportive Individuals

- Seek people who:
    - Listen without judgment.
    - Validate your feelings.
    - Encourage your growth.
- Avoid those who:
    - Minimize your experiences.
    - Dismiss your boundaries.
    - Exhibit controlling or manipulative behaviors.

5.2 Joining Support Groups

- Connect with others who have experienced gaslighting through in-person or online support groups.

- Sharing stories can normalize your feelings and provide valuable coping strategies.

6. Practicing Self-Care

Self-care is essential for physical, emotional, and mental well-being.

6.1 Daily Self-Care Routine

- Incorporate small acts of self-care into your daily life, such as:
    - A 10-minute meditation or breathing exercise.
    - A short walk in nature.
    - Journaling or gratitude exercises.
- Prioritize rest and proper nutrition to support overall health.

6.2 Creative Outlets

- Explore creative activities that bring joy and relaxation, such as painting, dancing, or gardening.
- Creative expression helps process emotions and rebuild confidence.

7. Cultivating Resilience

Building resilience equips you to face future challenges with strength and adaptability.

7.1 Reframing Setbacks

- View setbacks as opportunities to learn and grow.
- Reflect on past challenges and how you overcame them to build confidence.

7.2 Strength Affirmations

- Create a list of affirmations that highlight your resilience:
    - "I am strong enough to overcome challenges."
    - "I trust myself to handle difficult situations."

7.3 Mindfulness Practices

- Practice mindfulness to stay grounded in the present moment.
    - **Exercise:** Focus on your breathing for 5 minutes, observing each inhale and exhale.

8. Educating Yourself About Gaslighting

Understanding gaslighting empowers you to recognize and resist it in the future.

8.1 Read Books and Articles

- Explore books like *The Gaslight Effect* by Dr. Robin Stern to deepen your understanding.
- Stay informed about manipulation tactics to protect yourself and help others.

8.2 Attend Workshops or Therapy

- Participate in personal development workshops focused on communication and boundaries.
- Work with a therapist who specializes in recovery from emotional abuse.

9. Harnessing Professional Support

Seeking professional help can provide tools and insights tailored to your recovery journey.

9.1 Therapy Options

- **Cognitive Behavioral Therapy (CBT):** Helps reframe negative thought patterns.
- **Trauma-Focused Therapy:** Addresses lingering emotional scars from gaslighting.
- **Group Therapy:** Offers peer support and shared healing experiences.

9.2 Coaching and Mentorship

- Engage with life coaches or mentors to set and achieve personal goals.

10. Measuring Progress

Tracking your recovery journey helps you celebrate milestones and identify areas for further growth.

10.1 Keep a Recovery Journal

- Document your thoughts, feelings, and achievements regularly.
- Reflect on progress by revisiting earlier entries.

10.2 Celebrate Milestones

- Acknowledge and reward yourself for achievements, such as:
    - Setting a boundary.
    - Rebuilding a positive relationship.
    - Reaching a personal goal.

Journaling Prompts to Process Emotions and Gain Clarity

Journaling is a powerful tool for emotional healing, self-reflection, and gaining clarity in challenging times. Writing allows you to explore your thoughts and feelings in a safe, private space, helping you untangle complex emotions, recognize patterns, and foster personal growth. Here's a curated list of journaling prompts to guide you on this transformative journey.

1. Understanding Your Emotions

These prompts help you identify and explore your feelings, making it easier to process them.

1. **What emotions am I feeling right now? Can I identify their cause?**

- **Follow-Up:** How do these emotions manifest in my body (e.g., tension, restlessness)?
2. What is one situation recently that left me feeling upset or unsettled? Why do I think it affected me so deeply?
3. If my emotions could speak, what would they say to me right now?
4. What is one positive emotion I've felt recently? What triggered it, and how can I invite more of it into my life?

2. Reflecting on Your Past Experiences

Use these prompts to examine past experiences, their impact on you, and what you can learn from them.

1. Describe a time when I felt misunderstood. What did I need in that moment, and how can I provide it to myself now?
2. What is a recurring pattern in my relationships or behavior? Where do I think it originates from?
3. Think about a time you overcame a challenge. What strengths did you rely on, and how can you apply them now?
4. Is there a memory I keep revisiting? What about it feels unresolved, and what would closure look like for me?

3. Gaining Clarity About Your Needs and Desires

These prompts focus on understanding what you want and need to thrive.

1. What do I need most right now—emotionally, physically, or mentally? How can I start meeting this need?
2. What does a fulfilling life look like for me? Describe it in detail, including relationships, career, and self-care.
3. What are three things that bring me joy? How can I incorporate them into my daily life more often?
4. What are my top three priorities this week/month/year? Am I dedicating enough time and energy to them?

4. Exploring Boundaries and Personal Values

These prompts help you define your boundaries and understand what matters most to you.

1. What boundaries do I currently have in my relationships, and are they being respected?
2. Is there a boundary I need to set but haven't yet? What's stopping me from setting it, and how can I overcome this obstacle?
3. What are my core values? How aligned is my current lifestyle with these values?
4. Write about a time you felt truly respected. What made you feel that way, and how can you cultivate more of that in your relationships?

5. Processing Difficult Situations

Use these prompts to work through challenges and gain new perspectives.

1. What is one challenge I am currently facing? Break it down into smaller parts—what can I control, and what can't I control?
2. What advice would I give to a friend going through the same situation? How can I apply that advice to myself?
3. What is one thing I can do today to move closer to resolving this issue or finding peace with it?
4. If this situation didn't bother me as much, what would my life look and feel like? What steps can I take toward that reality?

6. Rebuilding Self-Esteem and Confidence

These prompts guide you toward recognizing your strengths and celebrating your progress.

1. What are three things I admire about myself? Why do these traits matter to me?
2. Describe a time when I felt proud of myself. What did I achieve, and how did it make me feel?
3. What are five small wins I've accomplished this week? How can I celebrate these moments?
4. What is one way I've grown in the past year? How can I continue building on this progress?

7. Cultivating Gratitude and Positivity

Gratitude shifts your focus from what's wrong to what's going well, fostering a positive outlook.

1. What are three things I am grateful for today? How do they contribute to my happiness or well-being?
2. Who has made a positive impact on my life recently? How can I express my appreciation to them?
3. What's one thing I take for granted but would deeply miss if it were gone?
4. Describe a moment from today that made you smile. What made it special?

8. Visualizing Your Future

These prompts help you set intentions and envision the life you want.

1. What does my ideal day look like? Write about it from the moment you wake up to when you go to bed.
2. Where do I see myself in five years? What steps can I take now to start moving toward that vision?
3. What is one habit or mindset I want to develop? How will it improve my life?
4. If I were free from self-doubt, what would I do differently starting tomorrow?

9. Practicing Forgiveness and Letting Go

These prompts guide you through releasing anger, resentment, or guilt.

1. Who am I holding resentment toward? What would forgiveness look like for me—not for them, but for my peace?

2. Is there something I blame myself for? Write a letter to yourself expressing understanding and compassion.
3. What is one thing I need to let go of? How is holding onto it impacting me, and what would life be like without it?
4. Write a goodbye letter to an experience, relationship, or belief that no longer serves you.

10. Nurturing Self-Compassion

These prompts focus on cultivating kindness and understanding toward yourself.

1. What do I wish someone would say to me right now? Write those words as a message to yourself.
2. How have I been too hard on myself lately? What would a kinder perspective look like?
3. What is one way I can be gentler with myself moving forward?
4. If I treated myself like a close friend, what would I do differently today?

Breathing and Mindfulness Exercises for Calming Anxiety

Anxiety often causes a heightened sense of alertness, rapid thoughts, and physical symptoms like shallow breathing and muscle tension. Breathing and mindfulness exercises are powerful tools to counteract these effects by grounding the mind, relaxing the body, and fostering a sense of calm. Below is a detailed guide to effective breathing and mindfulness techniques designed to ease anxiety and promote well-being.

1. Diaphragmatic Breathing (Belly Breathing)

Objective: Activate the parasympathetic nervous system to reduce stress and promote relaxation.

How to Do It:

1. Sit or lie in a comfortable position. Place one hand on your chest and the other on your abdomen.
2. Inhale deeply through your nose, allowing your belly to rise while keeping your chest still.
3. Exhale slowly through your mouth, letting your belly fall. Imagine pushing all the air out gently.
4. Repeat for 5-10 minutes, focusing on the movement of your abdomen.

Why It Works:

- Encourages deep, controlled breathing, which slows the heart rate and reduces tension.
- Helps you shift focus from racing thoughts to physical sensations.

2. 4-7-8 Breathing Technique

Objective: Regulate the breath to calm the nervous system and ease anxious thoughts.

How to Do It:

1. Sit comfortably with your back straight.
2. Inhale through your nose for a count of 4.
3. Hold your breath for a count of 7.
4. Exhale slowly and completely through your mouth for a count of 8.
5. Repeat the cycle for 4-5 rounds.

Why It Works:

- Slows the breathing pattern, signaling the body to relax.
- The extended exhale helps release pent-up tension and carbon dioxide.

---

3. Box Breathing (Square Breathing)

Objective: Focus on the breath to promote mindfulness and calm.

How to Do It:

1. Inhale deeply through your nose for a count of 4.
2. Hold your breath for a count of 4.
3. Exhale fully through your mouth for a count of 4.
4. Hold your breath again for a count of 4.
5. Repeat for 3-5 minutes, visualizing a square with each breath.

Why It Works:

- Synchronizing breathing with counting and visualization grounds you in the present moment.
- Reduces physiological arousal and stabilizes breathing patterns.

4. Progressive Muscle Relaxation (PMR) with Breath Awareness

Objective: Relieve physical tension by systematically relaxing muscle groups while focusing on the breath.

How to Do It:

1. Find a quiet space and sit or lie down comfortably.
2. Start at your feet. Inhale deeply, tensing the muscles in your feet for 5 seconds.
3. Exhale and release the tension completely, feeling your muscles relax.
4. Move upward, repeating this process for your calves, thighs, abdomen, arms, shoulders, and face.
5. Pair each muscle relaxation with slow, deep breaths.

Why It Works:

- Helps identify and release tension stored in the body.
- Combines physical relaxation with mindful breathing to enhance overall calmness.

5. Mindful Breathing

Objective: Anchor your attention to the present moment by focusing on your breath.

How to Do It:

1. Sit comfortably with your feet flat on the ground and hands resting on your lap.
2. Close your eyes and take a few deep breaths to settle in.
3. Shift your attention to the natural rhythm of your breath. Notice:
   - The sensation of air entering and leaving your nostrils.
   - The rise and fall of your chest or belly.
   - The subtle pause between inhales and exhales.
4. If your mind wanders, gently bring your focus back to your breath.
5. Practice for 5-10 minutes.

Why It Works:

- Redirects attention from anxious thoughts to the steady rhythm of breathing.
- Enhances awareness and acceptance of the present moment.

6. Counting Breath Meditation

Objective: Distract the mind from anxiety by concentrating on counting and breathing.

How to Do It:

1. Sit in a comfortable position with your back straight.
2. Inhale deeply and count "one" in your mind as you exhale.
3. On the next exhale, count "two," and so on, up to 10.
4. Once you reach 10, start over at one. If your mind wanders, simply return to the last number you remember.
5. Continue for 5-10 minutes.

Why It Works:

- Combines breathing with simple counting to quiet the mind.
- Provides structure to help reduce scattered thoughts.

7. The "5-5-5" Grounding Breath

Objective: Use breathing and mindfulness to quickly center yourself during moments of acute anxiety.

How to Do It:

1. Inhale deeply for 5 seconds.
2. Hold your breath for 5 seconds.
3. Exhale slowly for 5 seconds.
4. Repeat for as long as needed, focusing entirely on the counts.

Why It Works:

- Provides immediate relief by resetting the breath and grounding the body.
- Easy to remember and practice anywhere.

8. Mindfulness Walk with Breathing

Objective: Combine physical movement with mindful breathing to reduce anxiety and ground yourself.

How to Do It:

1. Find a quiet place to walk, such as a park or a quiet street.
2. Walk slowly and naturally, syncing your breath with your steps:
   - Inhale for 3 steps, then exhale for 3 steps.
   - Adjust the count to your comfort.
3. Pay attention to your surroundings—notice colors, sounds, or the feeling of your feet on the ground.
4. Continue for 10-15 minutes.

Why It Works:

- Integrates mindfulness into movement, promoting relaxation and presence.
- Combines the calming effects of fresh air and rhythmic breathing.

9. "Stop and Breathe" Technique

Objective: Interrupt spiraling thoughts and regain control in stressful situations.

How to Do It:

1. Stop whatever you are doing and take a pause.
2. Take three deep, slow breaths, focusing on each inhale and exhale.
3. Repeat silently to yourself: "I am safe. I am present."
4. Resume your activity with renewed focus.

Why It Works:

- Breaks the cycle of escalating anxiety by introducing a moment of calm.
- Creates a mental and physical reset in moments of distress.

10. Loving-Kindness Meditation with Breath

Objective: Foster compassion and calm by combining breathing with positive intentions.

How to Do It:

1. Sit comfortably and close your eyes.
2. Take a few deep breaths to center yourself.
3. With each exhale, silently repeat kind phrases like:
    - "May I be calm. May I be safe. May I be at peace."
4. After a few minutes, extend these wishes to others:

- "May [name] be calm. May they be safe. May they be at peace."
5. Continue for 10-15 minutes, focusing on your breath and positive intentions.

Why It Works:

- Combines mindfulness with compassion, reducing anxiety and fostering emotional well-being.
- Shifts focus away from stress to a state of kindness and connection.

Recommended Reading, Apps, and Community Resources

Recovering from gaslighting, managing anxiety, or navigating personal growth often requires guidance and support. Books, apps, and community resources can provide invaluable tools, insights, and a sense of connection. This curated list offers resources designed to empower you on your journey.

1. Recommended Reading

Books are an excellent way to deepen your understanding, gain practical strategies, and feel validated in your experiences. Below are must-reads across key topics:

1.1 Gaslighting and Emotional Abuse

- **The Gaslight Effect** by Dr. Robin Stern
  - **Why Read It:** This book explains the dynamics of gaslighting, its effects, and how to break free,

offering practical advice for regaining self-confidence.
- **Why Does He Do That?** by Lundy Bancroft
  - **Why Read It:** Focused on understanding abusive behaviors, this book provides clarity and tools for recognizing and resisting manipulation.

1.2 Anxiety and Mindfulness

- **The Anxiety and Phobia Workbook** by Edmund J. Bourne
  - **Why Read It:** This comprehensive guide offers step-by-step strategies for managing anxiety, including cognitive behavioral techniques and mindfulness exercises.
- **Wherever You Go, There You Are** by Jon Kabat-Zinn
  - **Why Read It:** A foundational book on mindfulness, teaching how to stay present and calm through life's challenges.

1.3 Healing and Self-Empowerment

- **The Body Keeps the Score** by Dr. Bessel van der Kolk
  - **Why Read It:** Explores how trauma affects the body and mind, offering insights into recovery through body-based therapies.
- **Radical Acceptance** by Tara Brach
  - **Why Read It:** Combines mindfulness and self-compassion to help you embrace your experiences and foster inner peace.

1.4 Relationships and Boundaries

- **Set Boundaries, Find Peace** by Nedra Glover Tawwab
    - **Why Read It:** A practical guide to setting and maintaining healthy boundaries in personal and professional relationships.
- **Attached** by Amir Levine and Rachel Heller
    - **Why Read It:** Explores attachment styles and offers tools for building healthier, more secure relationships.

2. Recommended Apps

Mobile apps offer convenient ways to practice mindfulness, manage anxiety, and connect with supportive communities. Here are some of the best apps:

2.1 Mindfulness and Meditation Apps

- **Headspace**
    - **Features:** Guided meditations, mindfulness exercises, and sleep aids. Great for beginners and experienced practitioners alike.
    - **Best For:** Learning mindfulness techniques to reduce stress and anxiety.
- **Calm**
    - **Features:** Meditations, sleep stories, and breathing exercises tailored for relaxation and focus.
    - **Best For:** Building a daily mindfulness routine.

2.2 Mental Health Support

- **BetterHelp**
    - **Features:** Connects you with licensed therapists for online counseling sessions.
    - **Best For:** Professional mental health support from the comfort of your home.
- **Sanvello**
    - **Features:** Tools for anxiety, stress, and depression management, including mood tracking and guided journeys.
    - **Best For:** Integrating cognitive behavioral therapy (CBT) techniques into daily life.

2.3 Journaling and Emotional Tracking

- **Daylio**
    - **Features:** A mood tracker and micro-journal that helps you identify emotional patterns over time.
    - **Best For:** Monitoring emotions and behaviors with minimal effort.
- **Journey**
    - **Features:** A versatile digital journal with prompts and space for free writing.
    - **Best For:** Reflecting on thoughts and processing emotions.

2.4 Community and Peer Support

- **Woebot**
    - **Features:** An AI-driven chatbot offering CBT-based tools and emotional support.

- *Best For:* Immediate, accessible help for managing stress and anxiety.
- **TalkLife**
  - **Features:** A supportive online community for sharing experiences and getting encouragement.
  - *Best For:* Finding peer support in a safe, non-judgmental space.

3. Community Resources

Connecting with others who share similar experiences can foster a sense of belonging and provide support as you heal and grow. Below are some resources to consider:

3.1 Support Groups

- **Domestic Violence Support Groups**
  - Contact local shelters or organizations like the National Domestic Violence Hotline for group options.
  - **Why Join:** Share experiences, gain resources, and learn coping strategies in a supportive setting.
- **Anxiety and Depression Support Groups**
  - Look for groups through organizations like the Anxiety and Depression Association of America (ADAA).
  - **Why Join:** Connect with others who understand your struggles and can offer advice or encouragement.

3.2 Online Communities

- **Reddit Communities**
    - **r/raisedbynarcissists:** A community for people recovering from toxic family dynamics.
    - **r/CPTSD:** Focused on healing from complex trauma.
    - **Why Join:** Engage in discussions, share stories, and learn from others' experiences.
- **Facebook Groups**
    - Search for groups focused on gaslighting recovery, anxiety management, or mindfulness.
    - **Why Join:** Find a tribe of supportive, like-minded individuals who share your goals.

3.3 Helplines

- **National Domestic Violence Hotline** (USA)
    - **Contact:** 1-800-799-SAFE (7233)
    - **Why Use:** Provides 24/7 confidential support and resources for individuals in abusive relationships.
- **Crisis Text Line**
    - **Contact:** Text HOME to 741741 (USA)
    - **Why Use:** Immediate, free support for anyone in emotional distress.

3.4 Local Nonprofits and Organizations

- Reach out to local organizations that specialize in mental health, domestic violence, or personal growth workshops.

- **Example:** YMCA offers community wellness programs, including therapy and support groups.
- **Why Join:** Access free or low-cost resources tailored to your needs.

4. Podcasts for Ongoing Learning and Support

Podcasts can provide valuable insights, tips, and relatable stories for your journey.

- **The Mindful Kind**
    - Focuses on mindfulness practices and managing anxiety in daily life.
- **Unlocking Us** with Brené Brown
    - Explores vulnerability, resilience, and the human experience with compassion and humor.
- **Therapy Chat**
    - Offers expert advice on mental health topics like trauma recovery and self-care.
- **The Anxiety Coaches Podcast**
    - Practical tips and techniques for managing anxiety and living a calmer life.

Conclusion:

Embracing Empowerment and Resilience

Gaslighting is a deeply insidious form of manipulation that leaves lasting emotional and psychological scars. It fractures self-trust, distorts reality, and erodes confidence, often leaving survivors feeling disoriented and powerless. However, this book has shown that recovery is not only possible but also an opportunity for profound personal growth and empowerment.

The journey toward healing and reclaiming your life requires courage, self-compassion, and intentional effort. As you navigate this path, remember that the tools and insights shared in these pages are not just about surviving gaslighting—they are about thriving beyond it. Here, we reflect on the key takeaways and leave you with a roadmap for long-term resilience and empowerment.

Key Takeaways

1. **Recognizing Gaslighting is the First Step**
    - By understanding the tactics and patterns of gaslighting, you've taken a critical step toward reclaiming your sense of reality. Awareness empowers you to identify manipulation, whether it comes from individuals, institutions, or societal narratives.
2. **Healing Takes Time**
    - Recovery is not linear. Some days will feel like breakthroughs, while others may bring setbacks. Both are part of the process. Be patient and

gentle with yourself as you work toward emotional and psychological wholeness.

3. **Self-Trust is Your Superpower**
    - Gaslighting erodes trust in your perceptions, but rebuilding this trust is essential for long-term empowerment. Through practices like journaling, mindfulness, and intentional decision-making, you can reconnect with your inner voice and regain confidence in your intuition.
4. **Boundaries Protect Your Peace**
    - Setting and maintaining healthy boundaries is crucial for safeguarding your emotional well-being. Boundaries are not about pushing people away—they are about creating safe spaces where mutual respect can thrive.
5. **Support is Key**
    - Healing doesn't have to be a solo journey. Whether through trusted friends, support groups, therapists, or online communities, surround yourself with people who validate your experiences, encourage your growth, and uplift your spirit.

Your Roadmap to a Gaslight-Free Life

1. **Reclaim Your Voice**
    - Speak your truth unapologetically. Gaslighting seeks to silence and diminish, but your voice has power. Whether through conversations, creative expression, or advocacy, reclaim your narrative.
2. **Prioritize Your Well-Being**

- Consistently invest in practices that nurture your mental, emotional, and physical health. Self-care isn't selfish—it's necessary for resilience and growth.
3. **Educate and Empower**
    - Continue learning about gaslighting, manipulation, and emotional health. Use your knowledge to empower yourself and, when ready, to help others navigate similar experiences.
4. **Embrace Your Identity**
    - Rediscover and celebrate who you are outside of the influence of gaslighters. Your values, passions, and strengths define you—not the distortions imposed by others.
5. **Stay Vigilant**
    - Manipulation can resurface in new relationships, workplaces, or societal interactions. Stay aware, trust your instincts, and prioritize relationships that respect and affirm you.

A Message of Hope

Gaslighting may have left you questioning your worth and reality, but it does not define you. You are resilient, resourceful, and capable of building a life that aligns with your true self. Every step you take toward healing, no matter how small, is a victory. Celebrate your progress and know that your journey is unique and valid.

As you close this book, carry with you the knowledge that you are not alone. Many have walked this path and emerged stronger, and so will you. The tools, strategies, and insights you've gained here are your foundation for a brighter, more empowered future.

Final Words

Gaslighting seeks to diminish your light, but it cannot extinguish it. With awareness, determination, and support, you can rise above the shadows and shine brighter than ever. You are not defined by what has happened to you but by how you choose to move forward. This is your story—one of courage, healing, and rediscovery. Write it boldly and unapologetically.

References

The following references have been included to provide credibility and additional resources for readers seeking to deepen their understanding of gaslighting, emotional manipulation, recovery strategies, and empowerment. These books, articles, and studies were consulted or recommended for further reading:

Books

1. **Stern, Robin. (2007).** *The Gaslight Effect: How to Spot and Survive the Hidden Manipulation Others Use to Control Your Life.* Harmony Books.
   - A foundational book exploring the dynamics of gaslighting and offering practical tools for recognizing and addressing it.
2. **Bancroft, Lundy. (2003).** *Why Does He Do That? Inside the Minds of Angry and Controlling Men.* Berkley Books.
   - An in-depth exploration of abusive behavior patterns and strategies for breaking free.
3. **Kabat-Zinn, Jon. (1994).** *Wherever You Go, There You Are: Mindfulness Meditation in Everyday Life.* Hyperion.
   - A guide to mindfulness practices for reducing stress and fostering self-awareness.
4. **Van der Kolk, Bessel. (2014).** *The Body Keeps the Score: Brain, Mind, and Body in the Healing of Trauma.* Viking.
   - Examines how trauma affects the body and mind and offers innovative therapeutic approaches.
5. **Tawwab, Nedra Glover. (2021).** *Set Boundaries, Find Peace: A Guide to Reclaiming Yourself.* TarcherPerigee.

- A practical guide to understanding and establishing healthy boundaries in relationships.
6. **Brach, Tara. (2003).** *Radical Acceptance: Embracing Your Life with the Heart of a Buddha.* Bantam Books.
    - Focuses on mindfulness and self-compassion as tools for healing and acceptance.
7. **Levine, Amir & Heller, Rachel. (2010).** *Attached: The New Science of Adult Attachment and How It Can Help You Find—and Keep—Love.* TarcherPerigee.
    - Explores attachment theory and its implications for healthy relationships.

Research and Articles

1. **Freyd, Jennifer J. (1996).** *Betrayal Trauma: The Logic of Forgetting Childhood Abuse.* Harvard University Press.
    - Introduces the concept of betrayal trauma and its effects on memory and perception.
2. **APA. (2017).** *Gaslighting: How to Recognize and Respond to this Insidious Form of Manipulation.*
    - American Psychological Association.
    - A comprehensive overview of gaslighting as a psychological concept and its impact.
3. **McNally, Richard J. (2015).** *Cognitive-Behavioral Approaches to Anxiety Disorders: Evidence-Based Applications.*
    - A detailed look at evidence-based techniques for managing anxiety.
4. **Walker, Lenore E. (1979).** *The Battered Woman Syndrome.* Springer.
    - Explores the psychological effects of emotional and physical abuse, including gaslighting, on survivors.

Web-Based Resources

1. **National Domestic Violence Hotline.**
    - Website: www.thehotline.org
    - Offers resources and support for individuals experiencing domestic abuse, including emotional manipulation.
2. **Crisis Text Line.**
    - Website: www.crisistextline.org
    - Provides free, 24/7 support via text for individuals experiencing emotional distress.
3. **Psychology Today.**
    - Website: www.psychologytoday.com
    - A hub for finding therapists and reading articles on gaslighting, trauma, and emotional health.

Apps Referenced

1. **Headspace:** A meditation and mindfulness app that includes breathing exercises to reduce anxiety.
2. **Calm:** A relaxation app offering guided meditations, sleep aids, and mindfulness practices.
3. **BetterHelp:** A digital platform connecting users with licensed therapists.
4. **Daylio:** A mood and activity tracker for identifying patterns and triggers.

Supportive Communities

1. **Reddit:**
    - Subreddits like *r/raisedbynarcissists* and *r/CPTSD* provide peer support for individuals recovering from gaslighting and trauma.

2. **Facebook Groups:**
    - Groups dedicated to emotional recovery, gaslighting awareness, and mindfulness practice.

Author Name: Dr. Evelyn Harper

Biography:

Dr. Evelyn Harper is a psychologist, trauma recovery expert, and renowned speaker specializing in emotional resilience and the effects of psychological manipulation. With over 15 years of experience in counseling individuals affected by toxic relationships, gaslighting, and emotional abuse, she has dedicated her career to empowering people to reclaim their confidence and sense of self.

Dr. Harper holds a Ph.D. in Clinical Psychology and is a certified mindfulness practitioner. Her innovative approach combines evidence-based therapeutic techniques with practical tools for everyday resilience, making her work accessible and impactful for diverse audiences. Through her private practice, workshops, and online courses, she has helped thousands of clients break free from the lingering effects of manipulation and find healing.

A passionate advocate for mental health awareness, Dr. Harper has been featured in leading publications and podcasts, sharing insights on overcoming trauma and building emotional strength. Her work emphasizes the importance of self-trust, healthy boundaries, and community support in the recovery journey.

When she's not writing or working with clients, Dr. Harper enjoys hiking, practicing yoga, and volunteering with organizations that provide resources for survivors of domestic abuse. Her mission is to create a world where individuals feel safe, seen, and empowered to live authentically.

Dr. Evelyn Harper's debut book, *Breaking Free: A Gaslighting Recovery Toolkit for Empowerment and Healing*, is a culmination of her expertise, offering readers a comprehensive guide to overcoming manipulation and rediscovering their inner strength.

Disclaimer:

The information presented in this book is for educational and informational purposes only and is not intended as professional advice. The author and publisher have made every effort to ensure the accuracy of the information; however, they assume no responsibility for errors, omissions, or any outcomes resulting from the application of the contents. Readers are encouraged to consult with a qualified professional for specific advice tailored to their situation.

All opinions expressed are those of the author and do not reflect the views of any affiliated organizations. The reader assumes all risks for the use of the material provided in this book. The author and publisher disclaim any liability for direct or indirect consequences arising from the use or interpretation of the information.

All rights reserved. No part of this book may be reproduced, distributed, or transmitted in any form without prior written permission from the author or publisher, except in the case of brief quotations used in reviews.

Copyright

© 2022by Dr. Evelyn Harper
All rights reserved.

No part of this book may be reproduced, distributed, or transmitted in any form or by any means, including photocopying, recording, or other electronic or mechanical methods, without the prior written permission of the publisher, except in the case of brief quotations embodied in critical reviews and certain other noncommercial uses permitted by copyright law.

This book is a work of fiction/nonfiction. Names, characters, places, and incidents are products of the author's imagination or used fictitiously. Any resemblance to actual events, locales, or persons, living or dead, is purely coincidental.
First Edition: [Month, Year]
Printed in the United States of America

Legal Notice

This book is for informational and educational purposes only. While the author and publisher have made every effort to provide accurate and up-to-date information, they assume no responsibility for any errors, inaccuracies, or omissions. Any reliance placed on the information in this book is strictly at the reader's discretion and risk.

The content is not intended to replace professional advice, including but not limited to medical, legal, financial, or other professional services. Readers should consult with an appropriate professional for specific guidance related to their unique circumstances.

All trademarks, product names, and company names mentioned herein are the property of their respective owners. Their inclusion does not imply endorsement, affiliation, or sponsorship. Unauthorized reproduction, distribution, or transmission of this publication in any form is prohibited without prior written consent from the author or publisher.

By reading this book, you agree to indemnify and hold harmless the author, publisher, and any affiliated parties from and against all claims, liabilities, losses, or damages resulting from your use of the information provided.

www.ingramcontent.com/pod-product-compliance
Lightning Source LLC
Chambersburg PA
CBHW071631220526
45469CB00002B/564